ALEXANDER C

'Tell a story to take old men from the fire and children from their play.'

Alexander Cordell 1914–1997

ALEXANDER CORDELL

Mike Buckingham and Richard Frame

CARDIFF
1999

British Library Cataloguing-in-Publication Data.
A catalogue record for this book is available from the British Library.

ISBN 0–7083–1488–0

Typeset at University of Wales Press
Printed in Great Britain by Dinefwr Press, Llandybïe

Contents

List of illustrations   vi

Foreword and Acknowledgements   vii

Prologue   1

Part 1: 1914–1945
Chapter One   2
Chapter Two   12
Chapter Three   20
Chapter Four   27
Chapter Five   36

Part 2: 1946–1965
Chapter Six   47
Chapter Seven   61
Chapter Eight   74
Chapter Nine   87

Part 3: 1966–1987
Chapter Ten   97
Chapter Eleven   104
Chapter Twelve   108
Chapter Thirteen   124

Part 4: 1987–1997
Chapter Fourteen   133
Chapter Fifteen   152

Postscript   162

List of Illustrations

	page
Alexander in wartime with a railway unit of the Royal Engineers	30
Alexander as an officer in 1942	39
'Grubby' in the uniform of the Royal Observer Corps	40
Alexander and Rosina at Shrewsbury, *c*.1946	56
Summer holidays, Borth, late 1950s	65
At Ubique, 1960	67
Alexander with his Singer Gazelle	79
Tidenham, *c*.1971	109
Wedding day, 1973	119
Barcelona, 1974	125
At the Great Wall of China with Donnie, July 1983	136
At the Chartists' resting place, 1988	145
At the caves at Nesscliffe, 1989	146
Hong Kong, 1990s	154
With Richard Frame, 1996	159
With Mike Buckingham, 1996	160
Relaxing at Wrexham, 1992	166

Foreword and Acknowledgements

A hundred different recollections lead to a cogent picture of the man who was George Alexander Graber, known to millions as Alexander Cordell.

His journey started in the steamy heat of Sri Lanka, then Ceylon, in the first year of the Great War, and ended when he was eighty-two years of age, after a triumphant progress along the highway of literary success, down a tiny mountain track near the top of the Horseshoe Pass in north Wales.

Many people were milestones along his way, and to those we have encountered thanks are due for recollections, photographs and documents which have gone towards the writing of this memoir. Blame for omissions or errors lies solely with the authors.

Madame Monique Girault was a friend of Alexander's for thirty years, and her research into the literary aspects of his work are as absorbing as her personal anecdotes. Trevor Rowson of Nantyglo was a boon companion of the writer, particularly on historical matters, as well as the lightning conductor through which Alexander maintained contact with his audience and his characters. Miss Dorothy Watkins of Abergavenny was a mine of information about Alexander around the time he was writing his best-known work, *Rape of the Fair Country*. Rob Edwards, a fine printer in the old hot-metal tradition, not only helped with the book but was a friend close at hand when Alexander needed him. John Bowring, the borough librarian of Douglas, Isle of Man, was generous with his time, and his contribution is gratefully acknowledged as is that of his staff. Roger Sims of Manx National Heritage contributed handsomely to our understanding of Alexander's Manx years.

Alexander had a great respect for librarians and archivists whom he rightly saw as keepers of the flame. We continue with this tradition and express fulsome thanks to the staff of Newport County Borough Council Library and to Torfaen Borough Council, several departments of which have been of assistance.

Moving north and across the border into England, we are grateful for the recollections of Mrs Gwen Bowen, her brother Donald Rogers, and also Mary and Vicky. Just as Alexander sat at their fire almost sixty years ago, so his memory warms their family home today. Also in Shrewsbury, Mrs Margaret Jones was vivid in her recollections of Alexander and of 'Grubby', who served alongside her in the Observer Corps.

Back into the country which Alexander adopted, Major Phillip Davies recalls as if yesterday Alexander as a young captain. On that day in Major

Davies's Conwy home which Alexander had recently visited there seemed to be a fourth person present. Gerald James and Eric White were our 'scouts' in Milford Haven.

The good humour and professionalism of Ceinwen Jones, editorial manager at the University of Wales Press, and that of her colleagues is warmly and gratefully acknowledged.

This book is offered not by professional biographers but by two friends of Alexander Cordell who nevertheless worked from a mass of documentary material. Out of affection and also to aid clarity, the subject has been referred to throughout as 'Alexander'. Alexander gave slightly differing accounts of many stories, most of which were never written down. The versions most often related are the ones told here.

Women had a special place in Alexander's work. Anne-Marie and Heather were also his friends. Great was their fortitude, especially when the authors were away on 'recce'.

One such reconnaissance mission led to an unexpected event which, to us, standing on exactly the spot where our old friend had died, seemed portentous. It was the day of the inquest. Weeks before, the police had been there to take his body away. The little rill ran as it had always run and the stout thorn tree curved and twisted by the winds of half a hundred winters hung like a question mark. If a spirit played around that place it was in the warm autumnal wind and was a frolicsome thing, for Alexander would not care to have grief around him for long. As he stepped across the stream, Richard looked down to ensure a good footing and suddenly caught a flash of silver in the setting sun. He reached down and fished out a steel pen. Both of us recognized it as one Alexander often carried in his breast pocket. We felt then, as we feel now, that this was a sign.

In the making of this book several things have happened to help us along the way. The book's completion, we feel, is not entirely of our own doing.

Mike Buckingham and Richard Frame
1998

Prologue

In the late summer of 1957, on a day bearing the first intimations of autumn, a rider, no longer young, dismounted from his motor-bike after climbing through high, cool cloisters of beech to a place above Govilon near Abergavenny, known locally as Fiddler's Elbow, where the road bends sharply. He was of no more than average height but appeared taller because of his slightness and erect bearing. The hair that projected like bundles of wheat from a parting over the left eyebrow was thick and had been forced into wing-like shapes by the pressure of the goggles, and his eyes were bright blue.

An observant watcher would have noted the slight stiffness in the man's walk as, having propped the machine on its side-stand, he walked away from the road, swung over the five-barred gate and dropped into the leaf-mould which for generations had been gathering on the track to Pen-y-Graig farm. The impression of a soldier on a reconnaissance was reinforced by the ex-Army binoculars hanging from his neck outside his buttoned coat and by the clipped military moustache. A military background would also have been suggested by the way he took in the lie of the land, viewing it not for its own sake but for what tactical advantage it might yield.

Some distance due south of Fiddler's Elbow, between the road and the farm, the man found what he was seeking: a stretch of smooth gradient revealed plainly where the old tramway which had once run though the rails had long ago been taken away. A century had taken its toll and there was little to see, but in the man's mind the decades rolled back and cables creaked and trucks clattered and banged. His inner eye saw other lines threaded all over the mountain, polished to quicksilver by friction and reddened by the glare of furnaces.

Men and women had toiled by the light of these fires and it was their story that he, George Alexander Graber, had come to write. As he walked back to his machine, kicked it into life, settled his goggles back into place and started back up the hill, the creative detonation that would lead to the writing of *Rape of the Fair Country* was being triggered.

Part 1: 1914–1945

Chapter One

In a spacious room in which every window had been thrown open to catch the faintest zephyr of a sea breeze, George Alexander Graber, son of Regimental Sergeant-Major Frank Graber of the Royal Engineers, was born on 9 September 1914. It was a humdrum event in the life of Ceylon's British military colony except for Frank and Amelia Blanche Graber, who gave silent thanks for the infant's arrival, a perfectly formed brother for the eldest child, also named Frank, and for his sister Constance. Downstairs in the public rooms of the Mount Lavinia Hotel, where the tea-planters and soldiers mingled, the talk was of the war against the Kaiser. Made fretful by the equatorial heat, the child's contribution from above the smoke-filled bars, thick with rumour and speculation, was a lusty bawl. Frank Graber listened to the bar-talk with mixed feelings. Certainly, he was a son of the Empire, British as a baron of beef, but those he met for the first time would sometimes remark upon the Germanic sound of his name and he would remember the family story of how his own father came from Düsseldorf in Germany and had married a Welsh woman.

Frank Graber was a brawny man with enough authority in his voice to make the toughest Sapper look lively, yet the mixture of cheerful insubordination was leavened with exactly the right degree of deference in dealing with officers that British non-commissioned officers imbibe with their mothers' milk. In the army of 1914 it was all but impossible for the soldier, no matter how talented, loyal, brave, cunning or obsequious, to break into the charmed and privileged circles of the commissioned officers. The caste system of the natives who thronged the streets would not have been so incomprehensible to the British if they had considered for a moment their own social structure. Birth, not ability, determined one's place in the military pecking order and this was something of which the young Alexander must have rapidly become aware, for it was to be a leitmotif throughout his life.

In the complex social structure of the British army a sergeant-major, particularly a regimental sergeant-major, held a unique position as the keeper of the holy flame of a regiment's tradition. Officers could be posted with a regiment and then posted elsewhere but the senior non-commissioned officers, unless there was a special reason, remained with the regiment as its backbone, keepers of the holy flame of regimental tradition. They were part of the system which was nowhere written down but which makes the British army the unique organism that it is. The one and only time Frank Graber failed to abide by the rules lay nine years in the future when in a burst of temper, he was to undo in a few minutes the career he had been quarrying for himself for many years.

Although it cannot now be established for sure from regimental records, it is nearly certain that when Frank Graber's posting to Ceylon ended the family did not return home directly but travelled via Egypt, which in those days was under British protection. From there Amelia and the children proceeded to Ireland, Frank's next posting, where there had been one of the periodic upsurges of Sinn Féin activity. While Frank's military duties in Egypt detained him for some months his family were settled into rented accommodation in the Falls Road in Belfast. Here, two things were to embed themselves in Alexander's memory, the well from which his literary images would later be drawn. The first was witnessing a knife-fight between two youths. It seems to have been a sectarian matter although Alexander would not have understood that. What he instinctively recorded was the violence and passion of it, the raw mixture of crudity and courage. He was half-repelled and half-fascinated, and the image of it was to stay with him for ever.

The second was a more subtle display of human emotion with its dangerous potential for passion and conflict. Why, or how, New Zealand troops should still be serving in Britain six years after the end of the Great War is not clear, but Alexander was adamant that the visitor to their married quarters, a Captain Wetton, was a New Zealander. Alexander's account of the Captain Wetton affair remained vivid, never varying in its detail as some of his recollections, especially in later life, were apt to do. 'Instead of eating at his mess down the road he seemed to have his big feet under our table. I can see him now, as handsome as Lothario and twice as hungry,' Alexander wrote in an autobiographical fragment. Frank, it must be remembered, was still in Egypt, so the officer's visit to the Graber home must have set the curtains twitching.

It was 'Oh yes, Captain Wetton', and 'Certainly, Captain Wetton', and 'Have another piece of cake, Captain Wetton', from my beautiful mother while Gran, who was living with us, gave him the evil eye. Although gentle on the outside Gran could be a terror in the soul and it was clear to me that she did not approve of this gentleman who, she said, should be somewhere else in the world fighting for King and Country, preferably New Zealand. As for me, I tolerated Captain Wetton in the absence of my wonderful father who was the spit and image of the famous Georges Carpentier, France's national hero, who had fought the great Jack Dempsey in July 1921 – the Gorgeous Orchid as they called him. I recall thinking at the time that neither of these boxers would have held a candle to my big father, but he would have to be bought out of the army to fight professionally. This New Zealand gentleman, however, seemed to grow on my mother, for I was hanging around the scullery one night while she and Gran were doing the washing in the copper boiler when I heard my mother's gentle voice. 'Don't be so ridiculous, Gran, he's only a friend,' mother said. 'Does the world have to stop because Frank's in Egypt?'

Alexander claimed that he could remember the conversation word for word. That is probably true. His memory, even well into his eighties, was prodigious.

'It does where you are concerned, cariad,' her mother-in-law said, adding, 'Things always begin this way. The fellow's lonely and away from home and you've got three kids, remember.' Pressed to the wall and alive to the tension of the moment, I listened for the hushed admission from mother that Captain Wetton was to visit that night. 'Aye, so I understand. But there's no cherry cake, for he's eaten the last,' Gran said.

'I tell you he's only a friend, Gran. Truly,' said my mother.

'Keep it that way, girl, or you'll have me to answer to,' Gran replied. 'This is my son's house' . . . and then she saw me there and bawled at me and I knew she was about to put the skids under Captain Wetton.

Alexander was never sure whether his grandmother had written to her son to warn him about Wetton or whether she had spoken to him personally.

Something happened because Captain Wetton stopped calling and I hoped that was the end of it because the neighbours were hanging on the walls like string beans and sewing their noses to the window and saying it was a scandal not fit for decent people with Frank being over in Egypt and it was a wonder Gran put up with it.

It was the spring of 1924 and Gran was boiling sheets in the copper and my mother was baking another cherry cake when through the door came my father in full uniform. I can see him now, bullchested and ducking his bright-curled hair under the door at the back. 'Where is he?', I remember him demanding and Gran spoke up, saying that the Captain was not coming. Some mention was made of a letter and Gran wiped her hands on a tea-cloth. At this my mother looked at her and accused her of telling Frank about the friendship, to which grandmother replied 'I warned you. Didn't I warn you?'

Out the house my father marched with my brother Frank pulling at his coat tails but he was shaken off and father went straight down to the New Zealand officers' mess where, according to reports, Captain Wetton was having his dinner.

In an area of closely packed terraced houses the commotion had everyone at their parlour windows. Meanwhile, the three children had adopted different roles. Frank, the eldest, driven by a mixture of embarrassment and fright appealed for calm. Constance, on the other hand, had been acting as a scout, reporting on Wetton's whereabouts to her father. Only Alexander retained a reportorial detachment. He may not have been at the actual confrontation, but heard of it from his brother or sister, or both. '"Where is Captain Wetton?" my father demanded, and a dozen officers raised their eyes from the table and the man at the top asked, "Who are you, Sergeant?"' One can imagine the shock waves caused in those days by the burly, bronzed man bursting through the door, a proletarian intrusion into the genteel life of the officers' mess.

'I am Captain Wetton', said the New Zealander, rising from the table. These were the last words he spoke before going into hospital, Constance reported, for he was dragged out of the dining room by the scruff of the neck with his knife and fork still in his hands and well worked over. Two mess waiters came running to the Captain's aid but had their chops slapped black and blue and a big gym corporal whom somebody had called for help was dropped for dead. Then my father came home and washed the blood off his hands while my mother, hysterical by now, threatened to leave him.

'Go to Hell', said my father.

It's very sad to see your parents falling out like that. My father walked into the kitchen waiting for the police to come and my mother pulled her hair down over her face to hide her tears. Gran sat in her big armchair, sick with weeping, saying God help everybody for it would end in a court-martial and that if she had known that Frank was going to act like a madman she would never have told him. In the kitchen, amid the stony silence of lost love, we sat waiting for the Military Police. I was watching my father with his big hands clenched together, I knew the simmering fury of him. The six of us sat waiting for the knock at the door.

But the knock never came. Alexander remembered the women weeping and the cold, heart-stopping apprehension every time a car was heard in the street outside. The Military Police car never arrived. Instead, Frank was told to report to Captain Wetton's barracks to be told that in order to avoid a scandal the Army had decided that the matter should be hushed up. Given the enormity of the offence of bursting into the officers' mess and severely beating an officer it must have been conceded that Frank Graber had acted under extreme provocation. The decision to fudge the matter was conveyed to Frank Graber by a padre – a minister in military uniform. Evidently Frank had continued with his confrontational mood for he accused the padre of wanting to hush matters up. The padre frankly agreed that this was the case. 'Easier for us, better for Captain Wetton, and also for you. Don't you agree?', Alexander records him as saying. 'A silence followed after which the padre explained that it had been decided to send my father back to England.' This solution may have been in the Army's interest and does not seem to have inconvenienced the New Zealand officer to any great extent but must have demanded very much more of Frank Graber, for whom a continued military career was now impossible.

The Wetton incident shows Alexander in an interesting light. He is in a family, but not of it: a witness rather than a participant. This ability to detach himself, to describe the mechanisms of family life without necessarily getting caught up in the drama himself was to serve him well, as his scenes of family life from *Rape of the Fair Country* onwards reveal.

An honourable discharge from the Army was arranged for Frank, and within a few weeks the Graber family was back on the mainland in digs in the London suburb of Shepherd's Bush. Using savings and Army pay due to him, Frank set up as partner in a building firm and almost immediately afterwards acquired shares in a billiards saloon next door to Blackfriars Boxing Hall in the East End. Alexander recalled:

This was a sinecure. The place flourished from the moment my father took it over. For me it was marvellous. It gave me licence to travel into London after school and at weekends and go next door to enjoy the company of old, burned-out boxers, the riff-raff of the profession, men brutal in appearance but indulgent toward a boy interested in their trade. This was a period in my life when I was determined to follow in my father's footsteps and learn the Noble Art.

At the boxing gym he met the likes of Johnny Curly and François Matchens, the Belgian featherweight champion who gave boxing lessons in his spare time to complement those given by his father. Throughout his life Alexander was to retain the love of boxing which was nurtured in his early years. 'I wanted to be a professional. My boyhood hero was "Nipper" Pat Daley, who was then being groomed for stardom. In those days the ring next door was run by the widow of Dick Burgh who had cut a swathe through the best middleweights in the country.' Hard scrappers and living well beyond the bounds of respectable society, these old fighters were innocents compared with Alexander Robb, whom Frank Graber had hired to run his billiards hall. Robb, from Alexander's description of him, was the friendly neighbourhood psychopath – charming, generous, plausible and utterly vicious.

I remember he was small and of slight appearance but later, when he was in Dartmoor he became one of the leaders and perhaps the main instigator of the mutiny in that prison. He was an enigma, who ran his little empire with an iron fist. My brother Frank used to travel to Blackfriars to pick up the takings or what we gleefully called the loot. Week after week Robb handed to Frank a bag of money which averaged out at over ten pounds, a small fortune in those days. No accounts were kept but such was my father's faith in Robb's integrity that neither he nor the partner in the business thought of contesting the payments. Later, this was the cause of some censure by a judge, for Robb was a small-time crook who was using the billiards room as a front for car theft.

Alexander had an interest in all sorts of human behaviour, including the deviance of the criminal. Such types, with their unexplained periodic abundance of cash and beautiful women on their arms, fascinated him.

Given her experience with the New Zealand captain, it is odd that Mrs Graber regularly invited Robb to tea. There is no evidence to suggest that her habit of dishing out cherry cake to anyone to whom she took a liking was other than a completely innocent gesture. What is surprising is that nobody commented when Robb turned up in a series of extremely expensive motor cars. 'He would take members of the family for a spin in his latest motor car which once, I recall, was a Page-Daytona, the sort of thing one only ever heard about being driven by playboys on the Riviera,' Alexander reminisced.

We were all pretty naive, I suppose, but we were all so completely engrossed in Robb's character. He was, or seemed to be, a beautifully educated man, and he became a regular visitor to the house. From his days in Egypt my father had interest in that country's ancient civilization which was tested to the limit by the knowledgeable Robb, so much so that my father asked a well-known Egyptologist to meet him. After half-an-hour in his company the expert announced that Robb's knowledge of the subject was profound. Henceforth, he said, he would be a patient listener while Robb expounded his theories of the ancient philosophies and riches of the kings of the Nile. In retrospect, we might have known that the manager of a billiards hall could scarcely have become the master of such a subject unless he learned it under peculiar circumstances. Later we found out he learned it all in prison. The bubble of our enchantment with Robb burst one day when my brother called for the loot and there was another man at the billiards hall also asking for money.

At this point it became nakedly clear to the Grabers how closely their lives had touched upon those of very serious criminals. According to Alexander, the man coming up the stairs ahead of Frank junior said he had come for his money, at which Robb replied, 'Here it is', and struck him a blow with an iron bar which sent him tumbling down the stairs. Frank dashed back to Shepherd's Bush with the news and warned his father that he was mixing with criminals. Despite this, there is some evidence that Frank Graber allowed Robb to run the billiards hall for a while before events came to a head. A police raid on the premises revealed stolen Rolls Royce parts in the garages underneath the premises and a warrant was put out for Robb's arrest.

Robb hopped it and was at large for more than six months before a police car parked in a lay-by in the Nottingham area saw a driver acting strangely and put the vehicle under surveillance. The car was seen by the policemen to stop outside a post office which aroused their suspicions. The driver got out and went into the post office and a few minutes later emerged pushing a railway porter's trolley with a safe on it. As the driver heaved the safe into the car and drove off the police gave chase. Robb's car was soon cornered by the police. He jumped out armed with a pistol and one of the policemen who rushed to disarm him was shot. The second policeman managed to overpower and arrest him. Robb was sentenced at the Old Bailey to twenty years in prison, ending up in Dartmoor where he later led the famous mutiny which would have been in the year 1930 or thereabouts, for which he received a further sentence. Ten years later Robb was dead.

The jailing of Robb ended a particularly unsettling time in the life of the Graber family when, for a while, they had employed one of the most dangerous and violent men in the land. Alexander was later to recall, paradoxically in view of his affection for the man, that Robb had looked like the notorious Doctor Crippen and had 'matched him in terms of evil'. 'Yet', he noted breezily,

nothing can erase the respect in which my family held him. With every opportunity to steal from us he always showed the utmost honesty, and when he died we mourned the passing of a criminal whom we thought of as a friend. An ice-cream was guaranteed from Mr Alexander Robb whenever I called in on my way to the Blackfriars club for a boxing lesson. He loved children, you see.

One might conclude that in a man who was prepared to smash another's head open with an iron bar and attempt to murder a policemen for the contents of a country post office's safe, that was just as well.

Alexander's life was not so much a jigsaw as a complex knot where one has to take hold of one end and follow it back to the other. An echo of the Robb incident persisted in Alexander's later habit of carrying a starting pistol in the door pocket of his cars. Such a pistol was found in the Austin Montego that he had at the time of his death. He also used to keep a toy gun in the house for the purpose of deterring burglars.

Alexander claimed that he had been mistreated by one parent or the other at various times, although the extent of this mistreatment was never made clear. Plucky by nature, the boy was relatively slight of build, which may have prompted some teasing from his burly father. In later years Alexander was to say that he rarely got on with his mother. Captain Wetton had cast a long shadow.

On 9 January 1925, the year in which Alexander was ten, his brother David was born in London. Alexander later remarked, 'I looked upon David's birth as a calamity since I had been the baby in the house. Now, with my nose out of joint, I watched him being changed and breast-fed and, to my consternation, was soon appointed his official nurse.'

At this time Alexander was attending St Stephen's County Council School in Shepherd's Bush where, on his own admission made in scattered autobiographical notes, 'I was supposed to be learning the "three Rs" but was interested in only one of them, which was writing. I began scribbling little stories in an exercise book, taking after my brother, Frank, by this time aged twenty, who was a junior reporter on a small newspaper, I think in Slough.' Alexander does not give himself full credit when it comes to the other two Rs. From early childhood a capacious memory was evident and right up until the time of his death he was able to quote, word for word, whole sequences of poems such as the *Rubáiyát of Omar Khayyám,* a favourite of his. Throughout his life Alexander was good with numbers, as the mathematical ability he showed when serving with the Royal Engineers was later to demonstrate. He retained an almost childlike delight in technology, taking with him into old age the enthusiasm for cars, aeroplanes and motor-bikes which had fired his imagination as a boy.

Poetry, though, was his first love, and young Graber's appetite for it was voracious.

On one occasion a master I hated, a Mr Guy, told us he had to leave the classroom for an hour and gave us the task of memorising the great epic poem 'Horatius' by Lord Macaulay. Upon his return he asked each boy to stand and recite as much as he had learned. I was the last to do this.

'And how much can you recite?' he asked me after the other boys had spluttered and stumbled their way through a couple of stanzas. 'Six verses', I replied gallantly. 'Really?' came the unbelieving reply. 'The best so far is two verses. Now we are going to see, are we not?'

I recited the verses parrot-fashion, in a manner which would have turned Lord Macaulay in his grave while Mr Guy stared at me in disbelief. Finally he put up his hand and said, 'Don't move! Just stand there. I'll be back in a moment', and ran out of the room to fetch Mr Knowles, the head, a six-foot string-bean with pince-nez spectacles, and a most kindly man.

Mr Knowles asked me if it was true I had learned the verses of Horatius and, having observed that Macaulay would have been delighted with my diligent attention to his work, bade me recite. I got to my feet and stood staring fearfully at him as he asked me to begin. I stood, unspeaking, my mind a blank while the rest of the boys glared at me. Mr Knowles picked up the poem and began to prompt me but I stood there tongue-tied while Mr Guy looked daggers. Time and time again the head prompted me with lads all about me clamouring to be heard by repeating the opening lines but nothing stirred in my now addled brain. It was one of the most terrifying moments of my life.

'But I tell you he did do it, Sir', said Mr Guy, and he appealed to the class which howled its confirmation.

I got the stick for it after Mr Knowles had gone for wasting the headmaster's time. As I was leaving the classroom at the end of the day though, the kindly Mr Knowles caught my arm and said that he was most intrigued by what had happened and asked me into his study to try again. I did so. Fourteen verses tumbled from me as if I had no control over them. It is a phenomenon I experience even today according to the state of the brain.

Sometimes the trance-like state could come over him when he was writing. Alexander remembered being seven years old and having just finished reading an account of the Battle of Bannockburn between the English and Scots in *Boys' Own Paper* when the demonic urge came to write his own version. 'Goodness knows where the words came from. They were just there in my head. They tumbled onto the paper as if somebody had been dictating.'

Chapter Two

Frank Graber celebrated the day of David's birth with an announcement that the house in Shepherd's Bush was to be let and the family was going to China. Reflecting upon this startling shift in the family's affairs, Alexander would say, 'That was the way things happened in our house. As fast as we would settle into one environment my parents would tire of it.' While that may have been generally true, the exhausted Mrs Graber, having just given birth, could not have been delighted to learn that within weeks it would be up sticks and away.

Frank Graber had signed a four-year contract with the Kailing Mining Administration to be the clerk of works building huts for Chinese labourers at Tiensin, a couple of hundred miles south of Peking on the Yellow River. Alexander's recollection was of the entire family decamping to Liverpool, there to await the sailing of the Pacific and Orient liner *Karmarla*. 'The event put David in the newspapers as being the youngest baby to travel 10,000 miles. As for the *Karmarla,* she was an old rust bucket and yet travelling on the same ship was the writer Somerset Maugham.' In 1925 Somerset Maugham was a writer at the height of his powers. He was a seasoned traveller, and his *The Moon and Sixpence* published six years before was an example of his preference for exotic locations. This was Alexander's first brush with a known homosexual. He later recorded, 'Maugham spent most of his time in the Far East travelling with his friend, paying the fare by his pen. Actually, I recall they ended up with us later, in Tiensin. I saw him there and went to speak but at the last moment I didn't dare.' Somerset Maugham was a revelation, a glimpse of what might lie beyond the closed worlds of the Army married quarters or the English suburbs.

Although Alexander had actually been born 'out East' he had no recollection of Ceylon. From the rails of the *Karmarla* he was seeing the East for the first time. It was in China that the boy was to discover his social conscience. At the time of the Graber family's arrival the country was a cesspit of corruption, banditry and murder.

An incident that remained vivid in Alexander's memory was when his father took the family for a drive in a new car and, by some error of navigation, strayed into a part of Tiensin known to be the haunt of cut-throats. Prudently under the circumstances, Frank was in the habit of carrying a loaded pistol in the car. As they tried to find their way home they were stopped by an armed gang. Fearing robbery and murder, Frank fired the pistol and sped forward, scattering the bandits, who, after they had collected their wits, fired back at the fast-disappearing vehicle. For some time afterwards the young Alexander was proud of the bullet holes in the vehicle and, one assumes, no less proud of his quick-thinking father. Often when describing this phase of his life Alexander was to write 'Educated in China by the Marist brothers. Attacked by bandits' – or variations on the theme.

It was always a matter of pride to Alexander that he had been educated by the Marist Brothers while in Tiensin. The Graber family was Protestant but contact with this Roman Catholic order would have added one more shade to his palette and a little more mystique. Alexander was to show a soft spot for the Catholic Irish (who, like the Chinese and Welsh, he saw as victims of English exploitation) both in his work and in his own life. Although an avowed atheist for much of his life, a pocket of residual Christian belief resisted all attempts at exorcism.

The dramatic shoot-out of which Alexander often spoke or wrote occurred in 1927. Much later, Alexander was to use China as a setting for several novels, reflecting the impression that vast country made upon him. Time and again, particularly in the latter half of his life when there was plenty of money for travel, Alexander and either Rosina, his first wife, or Donnie, his second, were to visit Hong Kong and once, by himself, he went to mainland China. His love of the country was reflected in the many ornaments with which he adorned his homes. Printed silks and elaborately perforated ivory were always much in evidence and his tables were carved from jade. When an ivory ornament – a ball within which was contained another and then another – went missing from his home in 1996, possibly stolen by a workman, Alexander was distraught although he usually paid scant attention to material possessions.

Chinese and Hong Kong friends were always spoken of respectfully. His attitude towards Chinese women was indulgent in the extreme; he idealized them as a combination of resilience and grace and would write about them with a special tenderness.

Sombre conclusions about Western involvement in China were there to be drawn but Alexander also had an eye for the amusing side of life. He was also becoming aware of sex and it was in China that he first saw naked women:

It was in a place called Chin Wang Tao, a coaling port where I'd gone with my mother on holiday and there met a Mr Song, a big noise in the Kailing Mining Administration with his wife and six concubines. Innocence must have been slipping away from me at this time for I noticed the sloe-eyed beauties always seemed to be smoking and were more than usually relaxed. One day Mr Song, polite to a fault, enquired of my mother whether the girls' smoking bothered her. 'Certainly not,' my mother replied 'I smoke myself.' Mr Song smiled. His ladies were partaking of the delights of opium. My mother was talking about Senior Service.

But smoking was nothing compared with the heady delights offered by a knothole under my bed. Some unspeakable cad had prised out the knot from the thin planking, thus affording an uninterrupted view of the entire room. What I saw there brought my puberty forward a couple of years, for I have never seen such a commotion of human flesh. Six full-bosomed girls were completely naked and engaged in a game of leap-frog. Calling myself all the swine in creation I knelt, eye glued to the hole. So transfixed was I that I caught the sound of approaching footsteps just in time, leapt up and flung myself back in bed just as mother opened the door.

'A little activity in the other room tonight?', she observed, matter-of-factly. 'Yes,' I answered weakly, adding my hypocritical master stroke, 'Sickening, isn't it? All that noise.' What a little prig I was!

'Are the girls disturbing you, dear?', Mother asked solicitously.

'Not in the least,' said I, hoping she'd exit quickly so they could bother me some more.

'Oh, well. Try and get some sleep, there's a good boy. I'll have a word with Mr Song.' She bent over and kissed the face of Judas.

It was an act of interference for which I never forgave her, for in the couple of seconds before diving back into bed, I had seen Mr Song, bare as an egg, his great stomach bulging, entering to applause and titters from the encircling concubines. The subsequent whoops of joy were a torment to me. I have no idea who caught on to my little wheeze but the next time I dived under the bed for more such entertainment somebody had blocked up the hole.

In sex as in other things Alexander was storing away experiences which would later be used in his work. Other incidents fuelled his growing sense of injustice, particularly as it affected the poor of China. One involved his father who, according to Alexander, began to argue with a rickshaw driver who had brought him home one night:

Father seemed to take exception to the fare and, in a rage picked up the rickshaw before smashing it down while the little Chinaman sat in the gutter crying. For this act of violence through which the rickshaw boy had lost his livelihood I was ashamed.

Shortly afterwards, in a second incident, Frank Graber did much to redeem himself in his son's eyes over the matter of foot-binding.

One of our servant's daughters was to have her feet bound, which first required the breaking of bones. The servant was crying. My mother asked what was the matter and she then told my father. I do not know whether threats were issued or money changed hands but the outcome was satisfactory. The girl's feet were never bound.

If China was to be a political initiation, something else happened as they were bound for that distant country which was to strike deep at Alexander's heart. His much-loved grandmother died. 'In fact', he wrote in a passage that may have been intended as part of an autobiography:

She did not die as other people usually do, but deep inside at the prospect of losing us and, what is more, at the prospect of going into a home. Her lively spirit came from the wild places of the Rhondda Valley and the threat of an old people's home quenched its fire. I recall thinking that my father – he whom she'd given life – had betrayed her by sailing East when her heart was so firmly planted in the West. I recall going to visit her in the home at Bushey, Hertfordshire, before we left for China and seeing my lovely Gran clutching a big black box which held her treasured possessions. She was lined up with a score of other grans also discarded by their sons and daughters. Henceforward these proud creatures were to be regimented into doing what they were told. She did not stand in withered apprehension but beaming, her rubicund old face lined with pleasure because she knew this was the way we wanted her to be. She took from her old black box a little trinket by which, she said, I should remember her. 'Rub this little brooch', she said to me (I later discovered that it cost sixpence from Woolworth's), 'and all your dreams will come true, my precious.' And then tears came into her eyes. Somebody said, 'Don't make it difficult, Gran', and I took her into my arms, hating them and thinking, 'Don't make it difficult! God Almighty! She was their source!' And then she put her fat arms around my father and said, 'Goodbye, son. May God protect you and don't sleep in damp sheets.' My brother and sister she kissed, also David the baby and then she came to me and with her face next to my ear whispered, 'Goodbye, my precious. May the baby Jesus bring you back to me', and then something in Welsh I did not understand, although I now know the word *cariad* for sweetheart.
  The nuns wrote and told us that she died on the second day of February when the frost was on the trees and Bushey Park a moody

skeleton of whiteness. It was our fourth day at sea. There are those in the world who should never be left alone to die. For seventy years she has been lost to me, yet there are tears in my eyes as I write this. I think I must have been pining for my grandmother all the time we were in China.

When Wall Street crashed in 1929, sending the world into an economic crisis, Alexander was fifteen years old and back in London and in his first job as an office worker. As he stood on the edge of manhood so the world trembled on the brink of madness. In Italy, *Il Duce*, Benito Mussolini, had gained power and Hitler was emulating him in Germany. The early part of the doomed decade was a period of marching and counter-marching by Communists and Fascists. Some men were in search of bread and work but many were in search of an ideal. Alexander's views were not formalized. Instinctively, though, he was a man of the Left, his political conscience having already been pricked into existence in China.

Alexander was not intellectually precocious and was unfamiliar with the literary developments of the age, which is hardly surprising given his youth and background. Later in life, he was to quote Ernest Hemingway with approval, but there is no indication that at any time during the 1930s he had read the emerging American writers among whom Hemingway was pre-eminent, nor Thomas Wolfe, Scott Fitzgerald or their English counterparts. Kipling, however, was different. For Alexander, as for hundreds of thousands of boys throughout the English-speaking world, the bard of Empire exercised a magical pull. In Rudyard Kipling's work Alexander found the exhortations to manly effort which were so much a part of a boy's upbringing at the time but also compassion, tragedy and irony. Kipling is not all 'blood and guts'. There is a compassion for the British soldier – Tommy Atkins – as Kipling refers to him. The poet's view of the British fighting man came to be Alexander's as well. A soldier might represent a corrupt regime or an empire based on exploitation but he does so because he can do very little else. To Alexander, the soldier fighting for an unworthy cause is no more culpable than an industrial worker whose labour capitalism is built upon. Anyway, the cursing soldier was manly, and if he sometimes had to settle matters with his fists, that made him all the more interesting.

Alexander's interest in the manly virtues during his school-days in the London area were not confined to what he could abstract from Kipling. Although only of medium height and relatively slight frame, he was proving himself to be a more than useful boxer and a devout student of 'the Noble Art'. Amateur boxing in those days was a much bloodier business than it is today in the few educational establishments where it is still tolerated. With light leather gloves and no head protection, bloody noses and cut lips were the norm, and the boxing ring was frequently seen as a place where a cocky boy might get his come-uppance. Alexander was certainly bright and boys being what they are, this almost certainly caused resentment. But many who tried to work out their resentment with a few satisfying punches to Alexander's already fine and rather aesthetic-looking features received a trouncing. In physical as well as moral and intellectual terms he was a doughty fighter, equipped with a dogged determination to battle on to the last round. Indeed, merely to live with a Germanic-sounding name like Graber meant that Alexander was often called upon to defend his family's honour with his fists. Frank Graber senior was pleased when Alexander decided not only to go into the army but to join the Corps of Royal Engineers.

In those days the trip from the Grabers' London home to Chatham in Kent, where the Royal Engineers' depot is located, took no more than a couple of hours, yet the short journey was more than the sum of the miles which clicked away beneath the train's wheels. For the first time in his life he had to make his way without the help of his family.

Then, as now, Brompton Barracks, which is the regimental depot of the Royal Engineers, stood gaunt and severe, not far from the naval dockyard at Chatham, square-built and solid as the empire which it had been built to defend. The year was 1932 and the Army from which Sapper George Alexander Graber accepted the King's shilling was in some respects still little different from the red-coated army which had defended Queen Victoria's realms. Conditions for the common soldiers were spartan. Home was barrack rooms containing two rows of beds facing each other across a centre aisle of highly polished linoleum. Each day the young Sappers, the Royal Engineers' equivalent of private soldiers, had to strip their beds and fold their blankets (sheets were an unheard-of luxury) into square 'bed packs'. The soldiers' webbing equipment and personal effects such as shaving equipment and soap would then be laid on the bed in a strictly prescribed manner. Any violation of the established kit inspection was punished by 'fatigues' or being confined to barracks. Life in the Royal Engineers was no holiday. With a million men of military age on the dole, the Army had no need to tempt recruits nor to make life more pleasant for those already serving. Much later in his life Alexander was to say that he was surprised when, on his first day in the Army, he was told to make his

17

bed in the same barrack block, the same room, indeed exactly the same bed-space as his own father had done twenty or so years before.

If the domestic arrangements at Brompton Barracks were designed to depersonalize the soldiers, the work and training schedules were equally dispiriting. Yet in this unpromising setting Alexander's instinct to set things down on paper came to the fore. Bridge-building, making tank-traps, demolition, laying and removing mines and erecting buildings all fall within the remit of the Royal Engineers – all very necessary in war but hardly conducive to the thoughtful life. Nevertheless, Alexander was indeed writing, a first faltering attempt at short stories and poems which had to be put down on paper wherever he could find some time or space for privacy and hidden away from barrack-mates for fear of the ribbing he would get if they were found. The exercise in subterfuge seems to have been successful. Writing to Alexander on 25 January 1983, Major Jack Phelps MBE, then living in retirement in Swansea, who had been an Army recruit along with Alexander said:

> I saw you on television the other night and it brought back memories of Brompton Barracks in 1932. Had seen you once before but was too lazy to put pen to paper then. I never thought of you as a writer. Always thought you would have gone for the opera or the stage. I remember you were always singing classics and light classics. Fifty years is a long time! I have a photograph of a suspension bridge party which I think includes you. I am taking a chance with this note and hope you get it. No more for now except that I was glad to see you married a Welsh girl. Kind regards, Jack Phelps.

The reference to opera and light opera is interesting because Alexander on only one later occasion and fleetingly, while he was living in Shrewsbury during the war, took any interest in the performing arts other than as a spectator or a potential writer of scripts. Light opera was probably a passing phase, undertaken perhaps for the amusement of his barrack-mates, although it may have been a way of signalling his growing interest in creative matters.

In 1932, at the age of eighteen, Alexander was at the peak of physical condition, his muscles hardened by the gruelling work of an Army Sapper. Matched to a naturally quarrelsome nature, this made him a determined and gritty opponent in the boxing ring. That year he represented the Royal Engineers against a visiting team drawn from three other regiments and won runner-up medal in the lightweight class. More medals followed when he led an Army team which vanquished opponents put up by the paper mills at nearby Aylesford. Stamina and lightness also gave him an edge in athletics and among the several medals he collected during those years and cherished to the end of his life was one for being in a winning relay team. The Army medals from the early 1930s were kept in their own leather box with only a few most treasured heirlooms to accompany them. In his otherwise undistinguished service as a Sapper Alexander had acquired a reputation as a fighter and had also began to cut his first literary teeth. A third acquisition was not a skill but a person. When Alexander met Rosina Wells who, in 1937, was to become the first Mrs George Graber, he was completely smitten.

Chapter Three

One weekend, flush with pay and bent on visiting his latest girlfriend in London, Alexander arrived at Chatham railway station and there saw a red-haired woman, somewhat older than himself, climb down from an arriving train. He never got to London. It was one of those moments he instinctively knew must be acted upon, an opportunity to be seized. Doffing his cap politely, but with the veins beating in his temples, he spoke to the young woman. Rosina was so surprised that she could hardly speak. She scanned the earnest blue eyes and, with her own heart thumping, permitted the young soldier to carry her bags out of the station and back to Brompton Barracks which he had left barely half an hour before. In one impulsive moment George Alexander Graber, a poor soldier with no prospects other than those to be gained by his quick wits, had bound himself to a woman who would be loyal to him for three and a half decades, who would bear his child and see him rise close to the pinnacle of literary fame.

It is possible that in Rosina Wells the young soldier saw the mother he felt he had never really had. She must also have seemed immeasurably wise and mature compared with the much younger women he had so far courted. Although an Englishwoman, from Hampshire, Rosina had auburn hair which gave her a Celtic look and her vitality did much to dispel any doubts Alexander might have had at the difference in their ages. He could hardly have failed to make a favourable comparison between her hair and the long auburn tresses his own mother had had in her youth. As was to be evident in his novels, hair was an important part of a woman's appeal, defining not only her appearance but her temperament. In Rosina's warmth Alexander found that which he had sought, but had not found, in his mother. He had loved but also feared his mother. Rosina offered a gentle love of which fear was not a component.

Her father was what we would now call a maintenance engineer employed by the regiment at Brompton Barracks, in fact a gardener and general handyman. Her precise place on the social scale must have been even lower than Alexander's non-commissioned officer-class background, although if she felt any class inferiority her clear, almost cultured, speech and bright intelligence concealed it. Short, in her mid-twenties and already tending to plumpness, Rosina must have seemed matronly in the eyes of most of the young soldiers. But beneath the benign exterior beat the heart of a woman who was not only to inspire

Alexander to passionate rapture but to nourish his emerging creative spirit. He bowled Rosina Wells off her feet. It was love at first sight. Certainly, his social skills were more advanced than was usual for a common soldier, and she may well have been surprised by his grace and way with words. All his life Alexander was to charm women, and their company always gave him much pleasure. This easy sympathy was to bring him a good deal of profit in later years as women flocked to buy his books, finding in them an understanding of a woman's mind that few other male authors were able to capture.

The liaison between Alexander and Rosina was not widely advertised among the other young soldiers, only intimates being let into the secret. At the time of their first meeting Alexander had finished his initial training and Rosina was working in service in London, travelling the thirty or so miles to Chatham at weekends and holidays. The first few months of the relationship were blissfully happy. Alexander was an attentive lover who never forgot the little niceties in those days long before anyone ever dreamt that such things would one day be considered patronizing. In those summers before the war, with unemployment still high, the young couple must have considered themselves more fortunate than most. True, there was little enough money on a Sapper's pay and Rosina's pittance from service, but the Kent countryside afforded many places for lovers to stroll, and beer and cider were to be had for a matter of pennies.

Alexander was for Rosina a witty and engaging young man, with an agile mind, a ready fund of stories about China and other places and a courtly and attentive manner. The two were absorbed in each other. In the wider world, however, titanic forces were stirring and were soon to intervene in their lives. Alexander, who was later to write about the Spanish Civil War in *To Slay the Dreamer* (1975), was barely aware of that conflict when it broke out in 1936. Similarly, Mussolini's adventure in Abyssinia, the Russo-Finnish war and German expansion in Europe barely impinged on his world. What, after all, was a young soldier deeply in love to do about these world events except partake of the fruits of his passion, walk and talk and read poetry and put to the back of his mind whatever it was the morrow might bring? But the War Office was not to indulge such an idyll.

In 1935 two shock-waves were to strike the couple almost simultaneously. That they survived them is testament to the strength of their love. The first was that whilst the five-year age gap between Alexander and Rosina was of no matter to them and may even have subconsciously been an attraction from his point of view, it was of great consequence to the Graber clan. It may have been that Mr and Mrs Graber had hoped for a daughter-in-law from further up the social ladder. The fact that Rosina's status was almost as low as one could get without being actually unemployed, combined with the age difference between her and Alexander, led the family to set their face against her.

The second event to interfere in their self-absorption was directly related to world events. At last Britain had realized that war was likely and a belated attempt was made to put the country's defences on alert. As part of this general shake-out Alexander was posted to Shrewsbury, the best part of 200 miles away and close to the Welsh border. The old market town, with its fast-running river and distant view of the Welsh mountains, must have seemed a strange and rather remote place. In its essence the town has hardly changed since the time when Alexander, in his off-duty moments, wandered through the alleyways between mellowed brick buildings, along the banks of the rushing river made turbid by the autumn rains, and across the Greyfriars Bridge, a light Victorian steel structure rather at odds with its surroundings. He would have wandered across the English Bridge and, at a time before his atheistic convictions were fully formed, into what is now the United Reformed Church which stands on the far side of the bridge to pray that he and Rosina might soon be together. During one such visit Alexander decided that this was the church in which he and Rosina would be married.

Among Alexander's comrades meanwhile, the main topic of conversation was the likelihood of war. The Spanish Civil War, precursor to the Second World War, was already raging. War would almost inevitably mean separation from Rosina. They would be married, it was decided, and furthermore, Alexander would leave the Army. Both realized that he would be back in uniform sooner or later, but his being out of uniform would probably win them an extra couple of months together. From the point of view of his career, Alexander might have done well to stay in the Army as part of its professional cadre and to catch the tide of rapid promotion as the hundreds of thousands of new conscripts arrived.

Although a practical man in many respects, he knew when the heart must be allowed to rule the head. He had already defied his family over the matter of Rosina and was not going to let the British Army now stand in his way. A telegram was sent to Rosina in London instructing her to hand in her notice and to join him in Shrewsbury. In the mean time he would begin the process of turning himself into a civilian, something that could be done with the minimum of fuss since his period of service was coming to an end. Resourceful and determined and with an Army trade training behind him, he did not find it difficult to get civilian work in the same line. A lifetime spent on the move meant that Alexander had a curious rootlessness and could contemplate major changes in his life without a qualm. It was something that remained with him until his dying day. Wherever he lived, and no matter how settled his life appeared to be, it was always a way-station on the route to somewhere else. His new job as a civil servant working for the department which maintained the Army's buildings was better paid than soldiering. While it did not place the couple in the lap of luxury, there was enough to furnish the basics of married life with a little left over at the end of the week.

Shrewsbury was the headquarters of the Army division which covered Wales and it was as part of his duties that Alexander visited Wales for the first time. It would not have been known to him at the time but Shrewsbury was also where the English army had been garrisoned at the time of Owain Glyndŵr in the fifteenth century. Very much later in his life, Alexander was to become spellbound by the life and actions of the Welsh leader.

On a motorcycle and with surveying equipment, he was sometimes sent far away into the Welsh-speaking parts of the country, a wet and chilly prospect perhaps for much of the time, but a glorious liberation when the sky was blue and the road dry under his tyres. With the looming nearness of the hills Alexander became more conscious of the Welsh blood in his veins. Beyond those hills was a world which was more ancient, with a strange and secret language of its own and therefore utterly compelling. Alexander's earliest encounter with Welsh-speaking Wales remained with him for the rest of his life. One day while riding enthusiastically rather than skilfully, he fell off his machine and ended up in a tangle of barbed wire near Trawsfynydd. An old shepherd ran to extricate him, but when Alexander thanked him in English the man merely grunted a reply in Welsh and walked away.

On 3 September 1939, as he listened to Neville Chamberlain's sombre words conveying the news that Britain was at war with Germany, it must have seemed to Alexander, only six days short of his twenty-fifth birthday, that he had been fated to go to war. He had been born in the same year as the beginning of the First World War and now a second conflict was about to break even as he gathered around him the ingredients of a settled and reasonably prosperous life with Rosina.

During these years their circle of friends had expanded to include members of the extended Rogers clan which ran a smallholding at

Haughmond, just outside Shrewsbury. On a bitingly cold day in January 1998, members of the family who had recollections of Alexander going back sixty years gathered to tell their stories. Each seemed to be able to throw some light on a different aspect of a complex character. As the distant Welsh mountains became backlit by the setting sun, Mrs Gwen Bowen remembered with great clarity how, in 1938, Alexander had come to the farm in the company of Frank Jones, her father's cousin's son:

> My Dad kept a gun and would often invite people over for a shoot – I don't suppose you would be able to do it these days but then anything you could shoot was a bonus. People were really rather poor. The Grabers often took something home for the pot.

It would have cheered Alexander to see that the family which had befriended him and Rosina during the early days of their marriage had prospered in the six intervening decades. The memory of Alexander is kept warm around the family fire. Mrs Bowen went on:

> Frank thought that my father would like a radio which he obviously wanted to sell and came round with it one day. Alexander said little but subtly tipped my father off not to buy the radio. I don't know what he thought was wrong but there was something. We were grateful though, for the implied warning. When the war came Alex used to pop up often to the farm to buy milk and eggs. By this time he was back in the Army. I think the headquarters of the unit he was attached to was at Coleham.
>
> Before they came to Shrewsbury Rosina was a nanny or a lady's maid. Rosina's father had been a general tidier-upper at the Army barracks in Kent. She had a brother who died in the First World War. [In fact it was after the war.] There was some tension in the family because of Rosina's station in life but Alexander said he would always stand by Rosina and would always talk to her father despite the lowliness of his job.

A curious incident occurred shortly after the marriage. When Alexander's mother came to Shrewsbury to visit the newly-weds she brought with her one of his former girlfriends. Mrs Bowen remembered the occasion well: 'It was a strange thing for the mother do. She and Rosina did not get on at all and this incident was not calculated to make things any better. Rosina went to her room and stayed there throughout the visit.' Having been so badly compromised, Alexander could do little else but seethe at this coldly confrontational act. Perhaps the fact that his mother had even devised such a scheme in the first place was a measure of her opposition to the marriage and starkly revealed that side of her character which so disturbed Alexander. There was no doubt in the Bowens' mind that, although social class may have had something to do with the Graber family's attitude, the fact that Rosina was older than Alexander also counted against her heavily.

The period during which Alexander was closest to the Rogers family was from 1938 until some time after the war. Donald Rogers remembered that Alexander was always looking for ways of making money.

> One of his wheezes was inventing a kettle which would tell you when it was boiling. I'm sure by this time somebody had already thought of the whistling kettle. I don't think he thought very much at this time about writing for money. If he did he never spoke about it.

Donald recalls that Alexander always seemed to have a motorcycle or a car.

> I remember him arriving in this car with a dicky-seat, one of the folding seats cars often had in those days. I think it was an old Austin. Alex wanted to take some manure away. My Dad said, 'I'll give you some manure', and proceeded to stack bags of the stuff in the dicky-seat. It smelt awful. I think Alex got rid of the car after that.

All his life Alexander remained quick to take a slight and could be inordinately proud of his cars. That Mr Rogers senior was able to pull such a stunt and still get a laugh out of him says much about Alexander's affection for the farmer. The manure incident may have been a joking revenge for Alexander besting Mr Rogers in a verbal battle over politics. 'Alexander was by this time pretty far Left and my Dad was a staunch Conservative. They would be at it cats and dogs, especially when Winston Churchill's name came up,' Donald said.

Donald's sister Vicky recalls a frightening incident which almost resulted in Alexander becoming a widower within a couple of years of his marriage. Old Mr Rogers kept a loaded shotgun near an upstairs window so as to be able to take a shot from upstairs at anything that might become a succulent addition to the pantry. Having become fascinated by the weapon while playing upstairs, Vicky picked it up and began to creep down the stairs.

I think I wanted to frighten Auntie Rosina with it. As I entered the room everyone turned to look at me. They were white. Somebody, I think it was Uncle Alex, rose to take the gun away from me but I must have got frightened and pulled the trigger. There was a terrible explosion and a flash and I screamed as the plaster in the room came down. When the smoke and the dust had cleared I saw to my great relief that Aunt Rosina and everyone else was all right. I had only intended to frighten her in fun but had ended up absolutely terrifying myself.

In 1998 the markswoman of sixty years before could not remember what was said to her afterwards but thought that being sent to bed without any supper was the probable outcome.

The Rogers's recollections of Alexander extend from when he was a pre-war civil servant through to his commissioning, and ultimate attainment of the rank of major. Early in 1939, Alexander was expecting to be called up for war service. When the call came it was to the Royal Engineers that he returned, although it was by now a very different soldier who set sail with his regiment for France.

Chapter Four

After two years in civilian life Alexander had already picked up some of the surveying skills that were now about to serve him well. The soldier who could not even achieve the status of a 'lance-corporal, acting, unpaid' very rapidly became a full corporal and very shortly after that a sergeant. In a few months he had reached a rank his father had striven for years to achieve. When Alexander first visited his parents with a sergeant's stripes on his sleeves the father had every reason to be proud of the son.

Alexander's field regiment was part of the British Expeditionary Force to France. The pain of parting from Rosina was only partly compensated for by the frisson of excitement that Alexander felt at marching towards a great and dramatic event.

A story Alexander always told was that he would have been the first British soldier of the expeditionary force to set foot on French soil had not a brigadier pushed him out of the way, thus claiming the honour for himself. One is tempted to wonder if the same brigadier was first off the boats when, a few months later, the British Expeditionary Force of which Alexander's unit, the 8th Railway, Coast and Operating Company of the Royal Engineers, was a part, was sent scuttling towards the Channel ports. The job of Alexander's unit was to requisition barges for the British Army and turn them into bridge pontoons, not the most glorious task in war but one to which he diligently applied himself. Calculations jotted in his diary indicate a grasp of engineering and mathematics far surpassing that which might be expected of a junior non-commissioned officer. Whether Alexander had ambitions to become an officer at this stage we do not know. What is certain is an awareness that his written words might have some message for posterity. His diary for 1940, a Collins' Engineer's Diary, survives and on 19 February Alexander made the entry, 'Rosalie (a pet name for Rosina) sent me a diary yesterday so from now on I'm going to keep a record of all I do while this damned war lasts.' A thrill comes with the very act of opening the old green leathercloth book with its calendar and conversion tables which remained in Alexander's battledress pocket throughout the doomed French adventure.

The first entries were made near Arras during the 'phoney war', the deceptive calm which settled before the full might of the German Blitzkrieg was unleashed upon the French and British armies. Rosina, like tens of thousands of other anxious wives waiting on the other side of the Channel for news from her husband, was almost certainly the inspiration for Alexander's first attempts to describe his surroundings in a quasi-literary fashion. The entries in pen are fairly easy to read. The pencil entries are not so suited to his stylish but not easily legible hand, and so transcription is difficult. An entry in the back of the diary begins: 'In the meadow, sweetly yellow . . . clothed hue of green, with the evening rain and sunset . . . the pretty . . . to green. Oh, it sets my heart a-flurry . . . the hills of yesterday, my footsteps homewards turning . . .'

In the main body of the diary for 29 February the mood is more rumbustious: 'Took 15 lads to the concert at [name not given, presumably for security reasons]. Lost my way back home and got in one hour late. Somebody wants to know if I can find my way back to the mess!' The next day is St David's Day but Wales is not mentioned. The diary space is filled with the opening act from Shakespeare's *Richard III* complemented by some of Alexander's own words: 'Spring is here and with it the deeper sadness of the days lost.' On 2 March he observes that it is a beautiful early spring day, beautiful not only for its sunshine and warmth but also because he receives a letter from Rosina. He muses: 'I wonder what the Spring will bring? Started the new 50-ton barge and work the only interest.' The next day the warm spell continues. Only anti-aircraft guns turned to the sky remind him of the war. With the wisdom of hindsight, we know that, during these spring days which so helped to soothe Alexander's feelings, a storm was brewing on the other side of the German lines. Evidently the Allied military commanders feared what was to come, for the pace of work seems to have been punishing. 'But it is no good howling. It will not shorten this blasted time,' Alexander wrote.

On Wednesday 6 March, the whole day's entry is a poem:

> Oh, memories of a sweetened kind
> I find in those a moment's bliss
> Of fragrant days that used to be
> The recollection of a kiss.

It is signed G.A.G. – George Alexander Graber – the first piece of creative writing to which his name is attached.

The evidence of the diaries is that the man who was to have a humanist funeral had, in 1940, a rather better opinion of the Almighty. The entry for 10 March, which was Passion Sunday, reads: 'His name was a great one – mine is impoverished and self-conceited . . . Sunshine for five days, lost days.' The poetic mood seems to have passed after a couple of days for Alexander is soon writing briskly about technical problems connected with his work. On pay-day, which was 14 March he went into town and bought some glamorous French lingerie for Rosina. Five days later he notes ruefully, 'Broke! Those pants are costing me something!'

On Easter Sunday there is a reference to Vimy Ridge which Alexander managed to visit during his none-too-frequent off-duty hours: 'No memorial to remember – only shell holes – trenches – cemeteries – unknown soldiers and the red ground. My heart aches for them.'

Deciphering parts of the diary, it is possible to trace some of the elements which were later to appear in *A Thought of Honour,* his first book. Sunlit fields, the sweetness of the breeze and the blue of the summer sky are all strongly suggested in the novel. Pay-day came round again, and on 30 March Alexander notes, 'Had too much last night. Singing "Macaushla", "God Send You Back to Me" and "Song of Songs" in the Middle Estaminet.' One wonders whether alcoholic remorse has added to Alexander's more general gloominess as he confides to his diary the next day:

Now comes a time of inaction, my dear. I have nothing to tell you. If I were to explain about the lonely and miserable time I am spending I would not be true to myself in any form in which you know me. Sometimes I think I should go to Norway – fighting for one's country and even bleeding for her would be a privilege and Heaven-sent in comparison to the dull boredom of waiting . . . I sometimes think my reason is leaving me.

And the next day, 3 April:

I lie awake far into the night and wonder what you are doing. I have built my existence about and around your sweet poetry but the words that fly to my heart and tongue do so little to ease the anguish of parting . . . I lie in golden cornfields with you at my side. I picnic – I walk and talk with you – you, my sweet, you are my complete dream and desire of all that I hold dearest to my sights . . . What is Spring to me – the Summer may come and go but I shall never see it. A great tree cannot grow without its sap . . . you are the heart and sap of my entire living and without you I cannot flourish. All is lost. I am as a tract of waste land.

Wartime with a railway unit of the Royal Engineers. Alexander was fascinated by all modes of transportation.

Even then the depressive vein is not exhausted for he continues:

I hate the days and dread the nights. The lonely hours of darkness serve only to renew my great longing for the nearness of you. If only it were possible to feel you warm and close against me – your naked body – the body I know so well pressed against my heart. It would serve so well to make easier this life of discontent and hatred . . . Never in my life have I known a period to be so dull and unworthy of the name of living. My heart stops beating when we are apart . . . I have no guide. I have no guide.

By 23 April, Alexander seems to be equating himself with St George, whose day it is:

St George's Day – the dragon is abroad again – in his wake he brings the misery of war, his nostrils breathe the flame of horror and discontent. The spear is in my hand and yet I cannot thrust – strange, inactive St George. You are too weak and you are swallowed in the maelstrom of the whirlpool boredom. Your sword is rusty and your powder damp – and you have no fair lady by your side.

It is interesting that Alexander makes much of St George's Day and so little of that devoted to the patron saint of Wales.

By 27 April Sergeant Graber is no more the lyrical poet but the tough, professional soldier, hell-bent on a night out on the town:

I spend a lovely evening – drunk coffee and ate beefsteaks with George Washington, George Cooper and Wimpy – I pay the bill. A lovely concert and a fight – what more could one wish? Bottles, a smack around the ear, a 'dead' Irishman, how silly of him to stick his chin out . . . ! Poor devil on a charge tomorrow. What he didn't say about sergeants generally isn't worth mentioning!

We do not have to tax our imaginations mentally to recreate that evening. In time-hallowed tradition a lorry-load of soldiers visits the local town, much drink is taken and a fight with another regiment ensues. It is as old as armies themselves, and Sergeant Graber takes to it with relish.

Retribution for the fight with the Irishman was swift in coming. The fight must have caused a major disturbance and perhaps some damage, for somebody obviously thought the matter serious enough to be reported to the military authorities. The diary entry for a couple of days later records that he was up before a Colonel Jasper and a Captain Thorpe whose adjudication was that he should receive fourteen days' field punishment. The Irishman he knocked down also seems to have been bent on revenge and even threatened to shoot Alexander. 'Threatened to shoot me! Ah, well, we'll have to wait and see. Have met Irishmen before. Everybody in the village agrees with me, so that's a consolation,' he cockily notes. The entry certainly suggests that the scrap was witnessed by a lot of people. Immediately thereafter the mood advances to one of flippancy for on 1 May he writes 'Call me early, Mother dear, and I will see the sun arise upon the glad new year – and I'll be Queen of the May. And that's all it means to me.'

Alexander's punishment seems not to have endangered his chances of returning to England on leave, however: 'Go on leave in June. Good Lord! However shall I last it out?' In fact the days of waiting, the listless and drab existence behind the lines, the routine of work, punctuated by boozy nights in the neighbouring town, were soon to end. In those days of early May a monster was stirring and St George, with all his proud gallantry, was to be no match for it.

In a tactical master-stroke, a German army greatly superior in training and generalship smashed into the British, French and Belgian forces, pounding all opposition into mesmerized confusion. Dive-bombing aeroplanes, co-ordinated with rapid armoured thrusts and the swift advance of first-class infantry, delivered maximum military power to the point of least resistance. British positions and airfields were overrun by a seemingly unstoppable flood of field-grey. Allied troops retreated willy-nilly before the Blitzkrieg, abandoning artillery, vehicles and even personal weapons.

In the space for 6 May Alexander writes after some words which are illegible:

> The place is ablaze. I helped four women refugees from D— [name omitted]. They had big parcels and were off to the station. Recall the English woman in the square at B—. Her son was with her. I asked her about her husband and the tears came to her eyes. She told me of terrible fighting and bombing and said she was speaking to five Tommies in a café at Br— before the Germans entered.

Refugees passed Alexander's rear echelon position, away from the war front:

> All told the same awful tale of an advance that was humanly impossible to stem. Planes swooped and machine-gunned our men from all angles. Nothing could be done, we had lost thousands. The Germans are flooding over France. The tide is against us. God in Heaven help us if we lose. I shall die rather than go home beaten even if it means deserting and joining with the straggling infantry.

And the next day: 'I cannot bear to die, leave my sweetheart, but she, I know, would bid me, as would my dear mother, father, brothers and sister.' Now, dramatically, Alexander's unit comes under attack from the air. 'They are over again – in the river this time,' he writes of a close shave during which he was forced to take shelter behind a river bank from the machine guns of a marauding German fighter-plane. 'No opposition. Our fighters are at the front. One of our drivers, Hornby, was machine-gunned with one of our colonels in a car yesterday and escaped, car wrecked. The refugees are pitiful, they come in an unending stream with fleeing soldiers, Belgian, French but no British. Thank God for being British!' It is interesting, given Alexander's general and lifelong aversion to jingoism, that the word 'British' is underlined and furnished with an exclamation mark.

Wednesday 15 May: 'Night on patrol. Town bombed and many killed. Saw the planes and the flashes. My heart goes out to them. The villagers are frightened. French losing ground. I wish I were there myself – it seems so cowardly to be back here. God help the boys at the front.' The immediacy of the jotted notes in Alexander's diary becomes almost cryptic as the German push continues nearer his own lines. On 17 May he continues: 'Today a massed retreat – evacuation of village – everything burnt – my God feel very near to heaven – my poor Rosalie! It is for her alone!'

The following day the Royal Engineers were forced back to Boulogne. Dispirited and bedraggled, they entered the town on 18 May. At the thought of Rosina, Alexander seems cheerful, although there is an odd quality to the entry which sounds like suppressed hysteria. 'Boulogne! Going nearer to my darling. The thought makes me happier. Must write or she will worry.' What follows is broken, but vivid, like a war-reporter's shorthand notes before transcription – the reek of burning houses and vehicles and the dusty, sharp smell of stone shattered by gunfire escape from the yellowing pages. On Sunday 19 May: 'Three air raids in the night – bombs within 20 feet of the rest camps. Horrible sensation – delayed action [bombs] too. Had to warn women to leave house. Never been nearer to death. I do not want to die – it means so much to my wife. Off to C[alais] tomorrow within 20 kilometres of the German front line.' And the next day: 'No, it is B[oulogne]-sur-Mer only five miles away a motorised column has broken through. We are to block the way.' A fighting retreat was in full progress and Alexander's unit had been ordered to delay the Germans for as long as possible. If he knew that he was caught up in one of the greatest retreats in military history, he did not dwell upon it. The reflective soldier-engineer was now, by pure weight of events, being forced to give way to the man of action. 'Gone the HQ intellectual! I am now an infantryman. I am in charge of a party of 38 men. We leave at once in lorries for Boulogne. Requisitioning cars to block roads. Terrible sights – human misery.' And with that entry, its very brevity seeming to capture the swift, tragic pace of the war, the diary stops.

What happened next was described by Alexander years later. Exhausted and constantly harassed by German air strikes, the British troops stumbled into Boulogne where, as was the case at Dunkirk, Royal Naval vessels and smaller craft, many of them captained by their volunteer owners, were gathered to take the raggle-taggle army home to safety across the water. Here on the wharves, Alexander and his men were huddled, waiting to board a destroyer. 'The Germans were coming down from the old town, firing at us all the time,' he recalled, describing the mass of men on the quayside, miserable but still maintaining some sort of discipline. A group of Germans was advancing under the protection offered by some barrels. Alexander took aim between two barrels and, as a German soldier emerged, opened fire. The German fell. 'I often think about that young man and the parents and girl-friend or wife he must have had,' he said remorsefully much later in life. 'I'm sure he had much the same sort of dreams and hopes as me.'

There is no independent evidence for what happened next, although he repeated the story several times and it varied only in its details. It more than suggests a growing egalitarianism.

The destroyer was at the dockside with its steam up and the men were waiting to get aboard but their officers had put their own kit aboard first. A young naval officer, a handsome fellow, was leaning against a gun, nonchalantly smoking even as the Germans were pouring down from the old town. He asked a soldier who the bags and baggage belonged to. 'The officers, Sir,' the Tommy replied. 'Is that so?' said the naval officer, grinding out his cigarette and strolling towards where the bags had been stacked. Then he began to kick them overboard. When he had kicked the last one into the harbour he said, 'Now the men can come aboard', and turned on his heel.

Alexander also spoke of a dying sergeant waiting to be taken aboard the destroyer. The man beckoned and asked him to write to his mother, which Alexander said he would do. The home address of a soldier does indeed appear at the back of a diary, just where one would expect to find such a hurried jotting.

An instant later Alexander himself was badly wounded. A shell from a German tank hit the stanchion of a crane near him, sending splintered metal flying in all directions. One of the red-hot shards tore into Alexander's thigh. Shocked and losing blood, he was bundled aboard the destroyer which pulled away from the quay with German bullets ringing against her hull. Alexander was given morphine and the Channel crossing was made in a drugged haze.

With scores of other wounded, he was stretchered from the dock area at Dover to a casualty clearing station for an assessment of his injuries. They were serious, their appearance made worse by the bloodied rags of his battledress trousers that had been blasted deep into the wound. Alexander was to say that eighteen separate operations were needed before the wound could heal. From the appearance of the wounds as they were revealed to the authors in 1996, it was clearly no exaggeration.

Unsurprisingly, given the extent of Alexander's injuries, there are no diary entries between 22 May and 17 June. But on that day a fragmentary and rather strange entry appears. The writing is thin and sketchy with a rather opiated quality, but a general sense can be made out.

Lovely to stand aloft as statues ['monuments' crossed out] its graceful spire . . . stood aloft . . . In my heart its place . . . I saw it first on misty morning graceful thro[ugh] the raining streets. And my heart was set afluttering 'twas my first day's school. But as the years have spaced apart its place is certain in my heart. Now it lies a shattered being of its former graceful life in the tract of cold destruction dusty 'neath a cruel malign. Small the Subject, small the . . . our discomfort. But my heart was proud . . . amid the city's hurry stood the spire with raised cross. Thro[ugh] its many turret ramparts run the pigeons high aloft. Gaunt its shroud, no shapely structure but my heart has ever yearned for its homely beauteous comfort.

Alexander had been moved to poetic language by the sight of a church spire and the doves fluttering around it. Whether it has any actual connection with his school is problematical. The fragment is of particular interest in that the first few words 'Lovely to stand . . .' hint at the Welsh idiom Alexander was to use in *Rape of the Fair Country* written nineteen years later.

Wales was to feature largely in Alexander's thinking at this time, the order having come through that he was to move to a place of convalescence there.

Chapter Five

Alexander always maintained that it was to Coleg Harlech, that academic outpost hard by the castle, that he was sent for his convalescence towards the end of 1940. In fact, while on an outing with Richard Frame in 1996, Alexander pointed to the neighbouring St David's Hotel and remarked that he was almost certain that was where he had been billeted. Viewed from the outside, the hotel seems to have changed little since 1940 when the Army transport which collected the hobbling Sergeant Graber from the railway station deposited him at the entrance backing onto the road into town. Seen from the sea-shore, the hotel is magnificent, with its bayed windows and balconies on seven storeys culminating in a rank of dormer windows looking out on the magnificent panorama of sea, rock and heath. Gulls wheel and scream, their cries echoing along the steep hillside behind the hotel.

On 15 November 1997, when the authors stopped at the hotel to take photographs, it was a buffeting cold day with memories borne on each moist gust of wind. The day before, Alexander's inquest had been held at Wrexham and his spirit seemed to be hovering around the Welsh places with which he had been associated. Richard Frame remembered the last time he had been in Harlech with Alexander. They had enjoyed fish and chips together. Eating in public places was one of Alexander's joys. A humble fish and chip restaurant, where he could watch people come and go, afforded him as much amusement as the most expensive eating place in Hong Kong or London. This day, with the summer visitors long gone and few vehicles passing, it was possible to imagine the khaki-clad figure being helped down from the Army lorry and picking up his kitbag, making his way past the sentries to the medical corps clerk at the reception desk.

At around the time of his convalescence Alexander read Robert Graves's *Goodbye to All That*. What he did not know was that Graves had occupied a cottage only a couple of miles from the hotel where he was to convalesce. By early 1941 Alexander was beginning to fix on literature as a possible career. It may be that a writer's life was in some way associated in his mind with the status of a commissioned officer. Although he may not have read Siegfried Sassoon or Wilfred Owen, he may have known that Owen had been born at Oswestry in 1893 and had studied at Shrewsbury Technical College before going into the Army.

Shrewsbury, some eighty miles distant, was where Rosina had remained. As often as possible given wartime travelling restrictions, she caught the train to visit her husband. The regime at the rest centre was by Army standards informal and relaxed and the non-commissioned officers, as they wandered through spacious, airy rooms with views of the wide sweep of the sea, must have felt that something of the air of the pre-war luxury hotel still clung to the place. During her visits, and as the long summer days mellowed into autumn, Alexander and Rosina would take gentle walks, a main topic of discussion being his plans to become an officer. Alexander's wounded leg was mending well. Although it would give him trouble for years to come, his mobility had returned. Since he was in a specialist corps there was no requirement or expectation that he would leave the Army on medical grounds. His determination to overcome the stiffness and pain was remarkable; a hill he pointed out many years later as being one he climbed in the autumn of 1940 would have challenged a completely fit man.

Some weeks after his arrival at Harlech, while he and Rosina were out for a stroll and had climbed a hill, Alexander was afflicted by a peculiar itching pain. He dropped his battledress trousers and was fascinated, and not a little repelled, to see a button emerging from his wound. At Boulogne the button from the grenade pocket of his battledress trousers had been blasted into the flesh and in the rush of the casualty clearing station had been overlooked by the nursing attendant who cleaned his wound.

On the east coast of Britain, facing German-occupied Europe, one could hardly walk anywhere without stumbling across military camps and airfields but on the quiet coast of Wales there were relatively few reminders of the war. Alexander was able to enjoy the undemanding routine of the rest centre where only a little light occupational therapy was expected of him. During his spare time he was able to lay plans for the advancement of his Army career and to discuss them with Rosina on long country rambles.

Early in life, Alexander had worked in an architect's office and he had developed some aptitude in that line of work. He in fact remained a quantity surveyor until well into the 1960s. Calculations in his war diary show a man who was quite at home dealing with engineering design, stresses and other aspects of construction. He had a strong mechanical aptitude and was at home with complex calculations. He also had a refined manner and, as a non-commissioned officer, had cultivated the habit of command. He was, in short, perfect officer material.

Three hundred miles away, a tormented Europe was suffering under the indignities and privations always imposed upon the vanquished by the victors. But in this quiet corner of Wales long walks, sea air and the time to think and plan all played a part in healing both physically and mentally. Alexander always said that China had shaped his social conscience but it was Wales that offered him something gently lyrical. Poetry seemed to be borne on the soft, warm westerly breezes, and the young convalescent was ready to absorb whatever a freshening breeze brought his way.

Poetry was in the air, but so, too, was ambition. As he strolled and mused, Alexander was translating the things he saw around him into words, describing to himself precise details of the physical world: the sun and stars, the sea and the way frost rimed winter's dead bracken. Monique Girault, a French teacher who forty years later was to befriend Alexander and to write a scholarly treatise on the imagery of nature in his work, observes that the moon plays a particularly important part in his later books. There is no doubt that images drawn from nature were honed and perfected during the Harlech interlude.

What was true of nature was even more true of men. Like a child prodigy unaware of the gifts that had been bestowed upon him, Alexander had always been a keen and instinctive observer of men and women, particularly their reactions under pressure. An instance recounted several times by Alexander happened several years before when he had been an ordinary Sapper. An illiterate soldier in his barrack-room had become the butt of the sergeants' and corporals' jokes, even though the non-commissioned officers' intellectual accomplishments cannot have been marked. One night, after being reduced to misery, the man had taken some soot from the stove which was the hut's sole source of heat and drawn a wonderful picture, full of figures and life and movement, all over one of the hut's whitewashed walls. It was an act of defiance but it was also an act of creativity. Sometimes when Alexander retold the story he was moved to the brink of tears. It remained a tenet of his belief that somewhere in the lives of even the most brutalized and brutish men, decency and an urge to creativity can be found. Every Welsh choir that ever sang, every working men's institute that ever yielded a college graduate, every haunting Negro spiritual and every act of solidarity between working men was for him a vindication of this view.

The year 1942 was crucial both for the war and for Sergeant Graber. The Germans were being defeated before Stalingrad and in the Western Desert, and America was in the war. In remote and timeless Harlech Alexander's plans were falling into place. In that year, after a short period of officer training, he exchanged his sergeant's stripes for a lieutenant's pips and, shortly after that, the three pips of a captain. The man who a

Officer and a gentleman: flanked by his NCOs and Sappers in 1942.

few years before 'could not even become a lance-corporal, acting unpaid' was now an officer and a gentleman, his 'other ranks' number 1869581 being exchanged for the six-digit officer's number 173530.

The extent of his injury made Alexander unfit for anything but a desk job, which was duly found for him at Shrewsbury. The home he and Rosina set up was at number 6, Riverside Close, Shrewsbury, a second-floor flat close to the river bank and away from the town centre just over Greyfriars Bridge. In January 1998, from across the river, the two-storey flats built in the 1930s looked exactly as they did when the Grabers were in residence. Overhanging trees and swans sailing elegantly by cannot completely conceal the semi-industrial nature of the district. Although the bridge and the Crown pub and the general riverside ambience give it something of the feeling of the Thames at Putney, there is a large factory just a few hundred yards down river, its huge brick chimney iron-bound and the face it presents to the river blank, windowless and stern, like a Victorian prison.

The middle years of the war saw Alexander living an almost civilian existence, leaving the flat in the morning and coming home in the evening and only wearing uniform while actually on duty. Mrs Margaret 'Peggy' Jones, a close wartime friend of the Grabers, who in 1997 was still living in Shrewsbury, says Alexander's wartime work never seemed to stretch him greatly. Given the extent of his injuries, it is likely that the time spent at Shrewsbury was an extended period of recuperation. Mrs Jones's husband Tom was an officer in the Royal Army Service Corps who had met Alexander in the course of his work. The two struck up a friendship which extended to their wives. Tom and

'Grubby' in the uniform of the Royal Observer Corps.

Peggy lived in a flat in Ellesmere Road and as often as not the couples were to be found in one another's homes. 'We played records and talked about things in general. At first I wasn't aware of Alexander having any particular interest in literature,' Peggy remembered.

He was immensely interesting to talk to and told us travel tales. I distinctly remember some of them being about China. As time went on we gradually became aware of an interest in writing. I was in the Observer Corps with Rosina and another woman, Phyllis Tribble, to whom the Grabers became particularly attached. Phil's husband, Bert, was a prison officer. Phil herself was very, very interested in amateur dramatics. They lived in Greyfriars Road opposite the school and not far from the Grabers. Bert had been a servant to the Duke of Connaught and at the time wasn't allowed to marry. They were wed secretly but the Duke found out and he was sacked. It was then that he went into the prison service and came to Shrewsbury. As well as being interested in amateur dramatics Phil also liked local history. I think she was a very great influence on Alexander at a time when his artistic side was developing.

The relationship between Alexander and Phil was extremely close. If Rosina was in any way concerned, she gave no sign. The atmosphere was one of general chumminess centred on talk about music and drama and on the daily chit-chat brought home from Observer Corps duties. 'We asked Rosina what she wanted to be called and she thought a moment and decided "Grubby". I suppose it was an odd choice, but that was her nickname from then on,' Mrs Jones said. Obviously the nickname was a jocular adaptation of Graber.

When all three women were present Alexander tended to be quiet, listening to their talk. Mrs Jones was certain that he had a particular interest in the way women communicated, both the content and pattern of their speech. Alexander would sit and listen, honing the style of dialogue he would later employ in short stories and novels.

Far away, on the other side of the country, the real war was waiting and it was inevitable that, given his military skills, Alexander would be assigned a part in the huge drama that was about to unfold. By 1942 American soldiers and war material were pouring into Britain. With GIs thronging the streets, and with tented and Nissen hut encampments springing up all over the countryside, it became clear that an offensive was envisaged, the logical consequence of which would be a landing somewhere on the coast of northern France. Just south of Aldeburgh in Suffolk, a highly secret Army testing range was being developed. Learning from their RAF colleagues, the United States Army Air Force had begun the bombing of Germany and the olive-green shapes of their B-17 and Liberator bombers left their condensation trails hanging in the clear blue East Anglian sky as Captain Graber reported for duty at the Orford Battle Area near Orford Ness. War, and the impending assault upon mainland Europe, was literally in the air. Alexander and his colleagues would see the sometimes badly damaged American aeroplanes come limping back and at night hear the drone of the massed RAF formations as British Lancasters and Halifaxes kept up the twenty-four-hour bombardment of Germany.

In the streets GIs were plentiful, lounging in their lorries and jeeps and wisecracking with the local girls. Alexander was to note that, while the American soldiers were rarely short of female company, British soldiers were usually without girls on their arms. This was little wonder when the Americans got five times as much pay as the British and were able to spend it upon a wide range of preferentially priced goods in the PX or Post Exchange which, as a purveyor of comforts to the troops, far outshone the British Navy, Army and Air Force Institute or NAAFI.

The Orford Battle Area was an enclave of British military activity, and immediately upon entering it Alexander was put to work on what were some of the most important technical innovations of the war. The 'Funnies', which also gave their name to the men who worked on them, were sundry devices that, when the invasion came, would go ahead of the main body of troops to explode minefields and bridges, and to smash down or incinerate obstacles. Many were built on the chassis of tanks and therefore the Royal Armoured Corps was to have an interest in them, but much of the development was the work of the Royal Engineers. Alexander was by now a captain, but captains were ten-a-penny in a place so over-run by 'top brass' and 'boffins', the senior officers and civilian scientists who constantly visited the Orford Battle Area to check on progress or to try out some new refinement. Alexander spoke of a senior officer who seemed to have taken a dislike to him. His superior required some spare parts to be picked up from Shrewsbury. So important were they that a car was to be made available to the officer charged with the collection. When Alexander was detailed for the job he was delighted. He would be able to collect the parts, deposit them safely and get away to see Rosina for a few hours. It was not to be. The senior officer knew his subordinate's wife lived in Shrewsbury but went out of his way to make sure that orders preventing Alexander from leaving the military establishment were carried out to the letter, with the driver ordered to report any infraction. Alexander had to spend a night in Shrewsbury only a couple of miles away from his wife and home. It was an incident he never forgot as being typical of the spitefulness and meanness often shown by the petty managerial class.

Not much documentary evidence exists from his period at Orford Ness, but there are photographs of Alexander including the one which appears on the cover of this memoir. With his field service cap jauntily sloped over his right eye and a wave of blonde hair erupting from under it, and his proud expression, Alexander looked the typical British officer. Already he had the moustache that he was to retain (though he occasionally grew a beard to go with it) for the rest of his life. He may already have been a champion of the working class but he was also aware that, in essence, he was no longer a member of it. In a photograph of Alexander on the footplate of an Army train, he is very much in command, with his hand on the controls and wearing an imperious expression. The common soldiers look lumpish and proletarian alongside this splendid figure.

Major Phillip Davies met Alexander at the Orford Battle Area where both men were captains, although Alexander had more seniority. In the autumn of 1997 the authors drove to see Major Davies at his home at Conwy, a large, white-painted detached house surrounded by luxuriant vegetation in the lee of a cliff. It was the day after the inquest into Alexander's death. Not long after Donnie's death less than two years before, Alexander had visited Major Davies and the two had chatted and reminisced in this very room. It seemed the ghost of Alexander was everywhere that day. We were hearing whispers from fifty-five years before.

'I'm pretty sure I met Alexander at the Orford Battle Area when the 79th Armoured Division was experimenting with new weapons. The 79th was specialist armour,' Major Davies said.

It was quite an isolated area where for several months the Funnies were being perfected. They got this name because the weapons were very odd. You had tanks which had fascenes that looked like haystacks on them. We had things called Congers which were used to clear minefields and also specialized armour. After Orford Ness we were sent to Fort George near Inverness on the Moray Firth. 5 Assault Regiment went there to train in embarking and landing and so on. I wasn't in the same unit as Alex. I can't remember exactly what he was doing but I was in command of a Troop. In fact, after Fort George, I lost contact with him because he didn't come across with us to Normandy. He had been hit in 1940 at Boulogne, I believe, and wasn't fit enough.

We were at Fort George nine or twelve months and didn't have much time for talking. We were working all the hours God sent. Some of the time we'd embark on Landing Craft Tanks – LCTs – and go out into the Firth with a naval escort with the tanks on board and we would be making towards Norway. I think it caused a bit of a kerfuffle in Norway because the Germans thought we might be coming. There was always an aeroplane overhead spotting you, and we would turn round and do a landing at Burghead. It was simply an exercise in amphibious landing, not a diversion.

Alex never talked about writing. The main thing we did apart from working all the time was have the occasional booze-up in the officers' mess. He was keen on that. He gave no indication of literary interest in the summer of 1943 nor did he talk over-much about Rosina who was in Shrewsbury. We had a second-in-command called Walker and I remember Alexander together with most other officers hated his guts. Alex told me he been sent on a job with men to get some stores or something from a place not far from Shrewsbury. Walker tried to check up on him in case he'd gone home to see Rosina. I never knew her.

We had a weapon in those days called the Conger which had been designed to clear a path through minefields. There was an incident, I think at the Orford Battle Area during trials, when a sergeant checked on the thing and it blew up and took his legs off. This made an impression upon Alexander. It was his and my feeling that the Conger, which involved nitro-glycerine, should never have gone into general service but it did, with the consequences I've just told you about. I always said it always killed more British troops than Jerries. I operated it myself three or four times and they always reckoned you stood a fifty-fifty chance of being blown to Kingdom Come. It was a ridiculous weapon.

I never saw Alex again until a year or so ago [1996]. A man who had been a Sapper living at St Asaph telephoned me to say that a man called Alexander Cordell had been over to lunch and had asked about me and said he wanted to see me. I asked who the hell Cordell was because of course I had known him as Graber.

Alexander's horror of the waste of life involved in the development of the 'funny' weapons is evident throughout the pages of A Thought of Honour, his first full-length piece of fiction. Tinkering with the 'funnies' was dangerous work but there was an intellectual freedom which Alexander liked. Major Davies recalled that any soldier, from the lowliest Sapper to the most senior officer, could put forward ideas. Alexander would have thrived in this challenging climate and there is no doubt that he threw himself into his work, just as he had done into barge-building in France. 'If you had a bright idea you could bring it up and we'd evaluate it and play with it and see whether it would work. Many didn't do this but quite a few did.'

When asked about the impression Alexander gave in his book that 'Whitehall boffins' would sometimes come up with suicidal schemes which the soldiers were then expected to try out at considerable risk to themselves, Major Davies replied:

I wouldn't entirely agree with that although I admit apparently pointless things did happen. On one occasion I remember a lot of concrete being built in the battle area and some boffins came along who were supposed to have invented some fantastic explosive. We didn't know much about atomic explosions although some of us might have been thinking along those lines. They were fiddling and faffing about with these concrete things for three or four weeks and I thought to myself you'd need the maximum amount of co-operation from the Jerries to take these things into battle. You'd have to send them a postcard to let them know you were coming! In the end I drew the short straw and had to fire the damned thing. We were in a farmhouse at a place called Scott's Hall which is a bird reserve at Middlesmere, crouched in a kitchen ready to fire this thing from a distance. I thought to myself that, if it was going to be such a mighty explosion as we'd been promised, the farmhouse roof would come down on top of us. I told the lads to get outside and dig a hole, and we shifted the wires and things to the hole whereupon there was a bang, but not a very great one like the old Conger had made. We didn't hear any more about this explosive after that and we didn't want to. It was a complete dead loss. What they thought they were doing I don't know.

Major Davies's recollection of the Orford Battle Area was very good and from the description given to him he was sure that the setting for much of *A Thought of Honour* was indeed this part of the Suffolk coast, just south of Aldeburgh. He remembered going on sprees with Alexander around the local villages or towns, and recalled a few fights:

He was quite aggressive. He took a swipe at me once when he was in his cups and I took one back at him. I can't remember what it was about. He'd had too much or I'd had too much, I don't know. You were under tension the whole time, you see. Most of the drinking was in the mess. Alexander was quite a hot-tempered bloke.

His recollection of Alexander's social skills in a more general sense was that he easily slotted into mess life.

He was an experienced soldier who fitted in very well as an officer. He certainly didn't seem to have a chip on his shoulder about officers and the relatively privileged backgrounds which some of them had. He was fairly typical, I would have thought. I didn't get any impression of strong political convictions. We didn't talk politics much during the war, although I was very surprised after the war when I found out he was so left-wing. The only politics we thought about was that bastard on the other side of the English Channel and how to get rid of him.

I didn't know anything about Alex's background. He was a room-mate and a pleasant bloke to be with even if he was obstreperous at times. He was senior to me and had a great deal of experience all round. When you think back, the rest of us were kids. In the assault brigade we were all young. If you weren't, you could never have stood the racket. After Fort George we parted company. I went down south to Waterlooville near Havant and then to somewhere between Gosport and Lee-on-Solent. I took one of the rear details over some days after D-Day and I was fiddling about in Normandy after that. We talked about those days when we got back together a couple of years ago. He would say what a shit so-and-so was or what a damned good fellow. It was always extremes with Alex. He never talked much about the early part of the war when he was in France, although I remember him saying he had been on the dockside at Boulogne and had been injured and there was a staff-sergeant next to him who knew he was dying. The staff-sergeant gave him his mother's address and Alex said he would go and see her and then something exploded near them and his jacket went and he lost the address. He always said he'd felt he'd let the staff-sergeant down.

The last part seems to contradict the evidence of the diary, where the name of a staff-sergeant is written in the back, but it is possible that the diary was misplaced in the months after Alexander's evacuation. The fact that no entries appear after 22 May, the date of his injury, supports that theory.

A year after Major Davies and Alexander parted company in 1944, the Allies had brought the war to a successful conclusion. Although many tens of thousands of officers were being demobilized along with their men, the years after the war were still highly class-conscious, notwithstanding the mood of the country reflected in the election of a Labour government. As the British Army of the Rhine was settling into German barracks to become a huge pool of bored soldiery just waiting to throw off its uniform and plunge into a new era of prosperity, Alexander began to make his plans.

Part 2: 1946–1965

Chapter Six

Less than ten years after first emerging from the army as a disgruntled Sapper without so much as a single stripe, Major George Alexander Graber RE found himself on a much higher rung of the class ladder with his material prospects greatly improved. A general consensus among historians is that throughout the Second World War the material standards of living for the greater part of the British public actually rose. Much of the work of slum clearance had unwittingly been performed by the Luftwaffe. As the British war-machine moved into top gear in 1944 there was actually spare industrial capacity which could be diverted into consumer durables. A glance at the *South Wales Argus* during the latter months of 1944, when British troops were still battling against stiff German resistance towards the heart of the Third Reich, shows bicycles and radios for sale in Curry's in Commercial Street, Newport. The war had changed economic conditions for good. There had been production lines for cars long before the war but their capacity was limited and they produced vehicles for the fortunate few. As the British war effort got into its stride these production lines had geared up to work at a hitherto undreamed-of capacity, turning out everything from tanks and aircraft, radio equipment, lorries and battle-ships to bootlaces. Economists well understood that the industrial genie was out of the bottle. Once production on this scale had started up it would be all but impossible to decelerate.

Alexander and Rosina must have imagined themselves passing from the darkness of war into some sunlit consumer uplands where the fruits of victory and perseverance would be theirs. The most obvious change in their circumstances was that Alexander was now an officer and a gentleman. The war had changed – perhaps for ever – notions of class and rank but some deference was still expected by those who had achieved commissioned status. On 4 January 1946 a letter landed on the doormat of 6 Riverside Close, Shrewsbury, addressed to Major G. A. Graber RE from the War Office. It thanked him for service to King and Country and confirmed that he was permitted to use the title 'Major' as a civilian. Egalitarian in many respects he may have been, but the young ex-officer was astute enough to realize that there was still some kudos attaching to a rank which had been attained through war

47

service during which, moreover, he had been severely injured. Throughout his life he was to continue to use his rank, although in later years he tended to reserve it for formal dealings and almost never in connection with his literary life. Clothes, holidays, furniture and good food were all now within reach of the young major. As part of its contract with the returning soldiers, the government found work for many in the public sector. Tens of thousands of officers who had served 'for the duration' flooded into the lower ranks of the professions. Alexander was offered a post with the War Office as a quantity surveyor, a skilled if somewhat tedious job. Its sole saving grace as far as he was concerned was the chance it provided to refine his literary skills, putting his life's experiences through the mill of his creative imagination and coming up with publishable stories.

There is no indication that the process of writing came naturally or easily, and Alexander was to admit later on that in the infinitely more competitive literary market of the 1990s he might not have thrived. After fifty years we cannot be certain precisely which story was the first to bring any literary income into the household but the stories that remain show little of the stylistic fluidity which was the hallmark of the mature Alexander Cordell. Also, his literary efforts may have been directed towards acquiring little luxuries rather than addressing posterity.

'Every time Rosina needed a new coat I would sit down and write a short story', he often said. His early efforts may have been for pin-money but his approach was professional. One can imagine the former major planning his assault on the 'cheaper feminine market' with the same efficiency with which he planned a military exercise. In those early post-war days women's magazines such as *Red Letter*, the *Oracle Library* and *My Weekly*, all published by the Amalgamated Press at Fleetwood House in Farringdon Street, London, had enormous sales. Any change in the women's market brought about by the war in which women had won some measure of emancipation was slow in surfacing, and the formula was still one of tall, handsome men with firm jaws usually clenching on pipes, with tweed jackets and comfortable middle-class jobs which they had achieved after having had a 'good war' – heroes rather like Alexander himself, in fact.

The earliest published story existing, although there may have been others which are now lost to us, was entitled 'The Gentle Wife' and appeared in number 1915 of *My Weekly*, on 26 August 1950. The introductory paragraph was corny in a very literal sense, and described how on this particular summer day the corn was gleaming russet-gold in the soft light, the evening was tranquil and the birds still, the cattle standing in little pathetic groups beneath the trees with their heads low and their patient eyes fixed on the farmyard. Somewhere lower down the hillside is Briar Cottage towards which John Summers, the hero, walks after a long day in the field. Predictably, there are lace curtains perfectly washed and hung and a little curl of smoke coming from the chimney. Summers's shirt is open at the neck, exposing the almost obligatory tanned chest and 'a battered pipe sticks out at an odd angle from his mouth'. John Summers may be a formulaic hero but the making of him came only after many months of patient experiment. Tall, bronzed and with a determined look he was the sort of hero women of the period expected to read about. The story seems to be unfolding quite predictably when, suddenly, the author makes us catch our breath. John Summers is wiping blood from his knuckles as he approaches the little cottage. Powerful physical violence has injected itself into the rural idyll. Summers has struck Tom Hodge, whose land he farms, and as a result has effectively dismissed himself from Hodge's employ. Mary, hearing this news, is the model wife, the woman to cling to in a stiff breeze. It will be a hard winter, she says, but they will see it through together, living off their own few acres. In time-honoured fashion John Summers, a man of few words, clumps out of the house, his pipe still firmly clenched between his teeth, to ponder his drastically changed circumstances. Mary is the precursor of many strong and loyal women who will inhabit Alexander's pages for the best part of half a century. Furthermore, some of the essential plot elements are present here. After he has left the house Summers bumps into Jean Hodge, Tom's daughter. Fearing a snub, he averts his eyes and prepares to mumble a greeting and pass hurriedly on but Jean engages him in conversation. There is some sexual tension. John has always admired Jean in some unspecified way. Far from being angry with him, she is chatty, and brightly says that her father was in the wrong and, anyway, it is the women who make the decisions in the Hodge household. She also dispels his fears about Mary possibly having had an affair. The man whose car had been seen outside John's cottage, she reveals, was innocently involved in the purchase of Hodge's land and was keeping Mary abreast of events. 'The Gentle Wife' is in the mainstream of story-telling convention for 'the cheaper feminine market' yet, in the space of a couple of thousand words, manages to give the reader a delicious thrill at the physical violence and the possibility of adultery. The scene-setting is excellent and the plot neatly tied at the end.

Wales is introduced into what is one of the oldest surviving examples of Alexander's work, a short story entitled 'Echo of Laughter'. The story is of a mysterious visitor who, one stormy night, calls at a cottage in Wales or the Welsh Marches, much to the consternation of the wife of the house who is alone. If Alexander crosses the border again in print before the publication of *Rape of the Fair Country* there is no record of it. The man who was to become famous for his works set in Wales was, in the earliest part of his career, notoriously reluctant to stray far from the Home Counties.

The years after the Second World War were salad days for the successful novelist. Ernest Hemingway had become a millionaire through his writing alone and, almost daily, books dealing with the theme of men under pressure or at war were coming off the presses. Perhaps Alexander realized that, although his contribution to the war effort had been as important as any, it could hardly be said to have been glamorous. After the escape from Boulogne he had spent all his time in the United Kingdom involved in the development of the 'funnies'. That he was rather defensive about this is indicated by the dedication of *A Thought of Honour,* which was 'To the soldiers who, in their obscurity, were not considered "Back Room".' Although he had been briefly under fire and seriously wounded, there were hundreds of thousands of men who had extended experience of combat in the air, at sea and on the fighting fronts, thousands of whom were capable of laying their experiences out in print. Alexander realized that it would be hard to find a niche in such a crowded market so he adopted a different tactic. By writing for women's magazines Alexander had found a solution not by going around the problem so much as under it, and plunged himself into what was the underworld of literature. It was an intuitive move that was to be the making of him, and he never forgot the debt of gratitude he owed to those now nameless editors in the late 1940s who, with the steady flow of rejection slips, also enclosed a list of reasons as to why a particular story was being returned.

'You know, most people read the rejection slip and throw it away or file it and any letters that accompany it are given scant regard. I always used to read these avidly because by studying them I knew exactly what the editors who successfully got material in front of millions of women readers were thinking,' he said many years later.

Alexander's quantity-surveying job was unchallenging and the peace-time Army not a particularly hard taskmaster. And it was an outdoor job. Moving from site to site he took in details of the countryside, its moods and weather. In almost all his work throughout a literary career spanning fifty years, Alexander made the weather almost into an ancillary character. His summers are lush with grass and heavy with nodding corn and with a somnambulant heat that bears down upon the characters themselves, giving them a more languid air and yet increasing their capacity for passion. Likewise, his winters creak with cold, entering the very bones of his men and women, although sometimes when the snow is on the ground they are playful and skittish. Snow in winter introduces the setting he likes very much: the kitchen with its bubbling kettles and boiling pots of *lobscows* and simmering *cawl* on the fire and the smell of drying woollen mittens and the sound of happy chatter.

From reading Alexander Cordell's books it is easy to imagine that he had always been saturated in the stories and life of Wales. In fact it impinged upon his consciousness very slowly. His grandmother on his father's side had been not only Welsh but Welsh-speaking and, although his affection for her was real, much of the influence he would ascribe to her was with the benefit of hindsight. During the tedious months which led up to the Panzer thrusts which drove the British Army to the French coast, he had thought only spasmodically about Wales.

He now had an army pension, regular civil service pay for a job which for the time being suited his temperament, earnings from short stories, an adoring wife, his health and good looks and admiring friends. Alexander had every reason to be satisfied with his lot as the 1940s opened out into the 1950s. If there was one faint shadow during these early post-war years it was that Rosina, approaching forty years of age, did not have a child. The Grabers' friends, Tom and Peggy Jones, had their daughter Julie, and Phyllis and Bert had their daughter Mary. For Rosina, the biological clock was ticking away at an inexorable rate. On 15 May 1949 at Shrewsbury, at last a child was born – a girl whom they christened Georgina, a friend for Julie in particular and the only child Rosina was ever to have. It may well have been this added responsibility that caused Alexander to move his literary ambitions up several notches and apply himself to the task of writing a novel the outline of which had coalesced in his mind and which emerged as *A Thought of Honour*.

In 1950 a colleague at work was asked if he would accept a posting to Abergavenny but for family reasons was reluctant. Hearing this, Alexander volunteered. He was the first to venture south to find accommodation, which he did at The Lodge, Llanellen, near Abergavenny. In the following weeks Rosina and Georgina joined him. After the riverside flat in Shrewsbury, The Lodge was the last word in rusticity. A little post office and shop form the public face of the village but The Lodge stands a little way back on the road to Llanfoist.

Happy though they had been in Shrewsbury, familiarity with its streets and surrounding countryside had bred a certain weariness. Here was a new playground for Georgina and a fresh place for the inquisitive Alexander to explore. With his quick ear, Alexander picked up the local speech. Although at first he may have been regarded as the 'young Major in The Lodge, something quite important with the War Office', he was a ready mixer, eager to hear the stories of these country folk. Inevitably, many of the stories centred on the Blorenge, the ridge of which forms the boundary between the Monmouthshire of the industrial valleys and that of the farmed lowlands. In Shrewsbury Alexander had looked towards the Welsh mountains and their mysterious promise. Now he was living on the shoulder of one such mountain. As he tramped its flanks either with his family or alone, its spell grew upon him, a spell which was to hold him in its thrall until the last days of his life. Of all the places his life had taken him, from China to Ireland and from Ceylon to the north of Scotland, it was to be this mountain that was to mean most to him. His first step on the sheep-cropped turf was to be the first in a long journey that would lead to international literary acclaim and no small degree of wealth.

The relationship between Alexander and this part of south Wales had yet to mature and deepen. In the mean time, though, he was content to explore its more superficial aspects. The family picnicked and walked all over the area, enjoying that 1950s pastime which is lost to us now – driving out to a country inn for a couple of drinks on a warm summer's evening while the children played nearby or sat in the car, smelling the warmth of the leather and longing for the next packet of crisps with its soggy blue bag of salt. Short stories were still flowing from Alexander's typewriter.

In 1952 Alexander wrote an unpublished 28,000 word treatise entitled 'Writing for the Cheaper Feminine Market'. 'Man is born to create,' he says rather grandly on the first page:

And the modern age is one which demands much self-expression. Hand in hand with the need for expression has come the less artistic need to reimburse incomes. Times are harder for a greater number of people. Print means money and a populace with a higher intellectual standard has turned to it for help. The age has produced a vast army of freelance writers who are bombarding the presses with great collective effort but very little individual success. Now, the embryo freelance invariably makes the mistake of directing his attack at publications so well served by the established writers that they have virtually become a 'closed shop'. On and on the beginner goes, accepting rejection slips stoically until, inevitably, he learns that the business of selling words is harder than it appears. Despite the entreaties of friends who assert that the road to fame in the world of letters is fraught with rejection, he ceases to write. What might have proved a good author is lost to posterity.

It is a rather wordy homily yet we are drawn to the central message. The publication, itself as long as a short novel, serves as an excellent guide to the craft of writing. All his life Alexander Cordell remained a debunker of those who sat at a typewriter with high-flown ideas about their calling. He remained, at heart, a humble man.

No teacher can offer a magic wand. In all learning a large responsibility must be accepted by the pupil. Therefore a notebook should be kept handy and the information recorded and applied practically with a degree of commonsense. The reader who believes himself to be an undiscovered Maugham or Shaw has done well to read this book so far but he is advised to close it now. The reader with classical literary ambitions must seek education elsewhere.

It need not surprise us that Alexander refers throughout to the cadet author as 'he', at no point adopting the feminine pronoun. The first example of a 'classical' writer which comes to his mind is Somerset Maugham whom he had met on the boat to China while still a boy. 'Writing for the Cheaper Feminine Market' is a practical little hand-book in which one detects the guiding hand of Frank, Alexander's older brother. Later in life Alexander was to bemoan the fact that Frank never had any creative talent and yet his help at this early stage of Alexander's writing career is acknowledged in several short stories. In order to increase the dramatic effect of his stories, especially those with a racy, dangerous, Buchanesque feel to them, Alexander would often append the by-line 'By Major George Graber, as told to Frank Graber' – the implication being that one brother had breathlessly told his tale of derring-do to the other, who had noted it down in fresh, vivid language for posterity. In fact, Frank had started life as a reporter on weekly newspapers in the south of England and in these early post-war years was a sub-editor on the *Financial Times*. Then, as now, this paper was at the forefront of financial and economic reporting, its distinctive pink pages recognizable on news-stands in every financial centre from Tokyo to Frankfurt. To become a sub-editor on such a publication Frank must have been somewhat more than a drudge working away on the very lowest slopes of journalistic activity. Indeed, it seems he was able to give his brother advice not only about the practical side of writing (always carry a notebook and capture the essence of a situation by jotting it down quickly) but also about grammar, construction and even plotting. Four or five years after 'Writing for the Cheaper Feminine Market', when *Rape of the Fair Country* was brewing in his mind, Alexander would listen carefully to the cadences of Welsh speech before committing dialogue to paper. This excellent advice had been given to him by Frank. Alexander's inversions in Welsh dialogue, which some modern readers find tedious ('Terrible it was that night . . .' etc.) had been used by previous writers but still had some mileage in it as a way of conveying the idea of Welsh speech and its rhythms. The commercial reasoning contained in chapter one of 'Writing for the Cheaper Feminine Market' reveals just how well Alexander had done his market research. Eighty per cent of the magazines on the newsagents' shelves were aimed at the feminine market, he claimed. The percentage is rather on the high side but in an age when 'do it yourself' was yet to become a national pastime and the leisure and sporting markets were less developed, the general observation was correct. The modern woman, he said, was a voracious reader, even more so than her Victorian grandmother. Rich or poor, married or single, 'from the countess to the humble mill girl (bless her), their literary requirements are catered for by an astute commercialism which long ago realized that women had displaced men as the readers of popular magazines'. His references to the market are not always flattering, at one point describing woman as a 'female Frankenstein which must be fed', but generally he sees the writer as the wooer, the seducer with a story to tell. The woman is 'a fickle lover; a mistress who, with a sigh, can transport an editorial dividend or prostrate it with a groan'. Very early on in his treatise Alexander warns that the duty of the writer is to put saleable material in front of the editor and to study the house-style of the magazine. All his life he read and studied women's magazines, consciously tuning in to the female reader's wavelength.

There is a current school of thought which protests that editors in this market do not read all the material sent to them. Do not be misled by a statement which is merely a salve to those embittered by constant rejections . . . of course editors read stories. They read them because it is their business.

The whole strategy is contained in his observation that, while one might earn a lot more for a story submitted to *Lady*, the chances of publication in that august magazine are slight, since one would be competing against top-notch writers. 'You cannot hit the bull if you aim for the sky . . . in the cheaper market the competition is strong but the quality is lower. It is precisely for that reason that I am concentrating on the cheaper market.'

Alexander had also hit upon another economic truth which was that while profits for magazine publishers were recovering nicely from the wartime low and revenue from advertising of new products and services which had been unavailable before the war promised even greater profits, little if any of this had filtered down to the writer. It was still, as before the war, a matter of words chasing the money rather than the other way round. This state of affairs, he said, would continue until writers banded themselves in a workable trade union and 'refused to write like machines for trash money'. The figures Alexander gave make an interesting footnote. While average earnings had doubled since the end of the war (the treatise was written in 1952), incomes for writers had remained at pre-war levels: thirty shillings (£1.50) per thousand words for the cheaper end of the market and £2 a thousand for serials. The aspiring modern writer may give a tired smile of recognition at these words, although many will find the following assertion somewhat incredible: 'While editors are bound to certain rates by their publishers they try hard to make up for it by promptness of payment.' One wonders if this remark was made to butter up editors who had been helpful to him in the past and with whom he wished to deal in the future, for he continued: 'Editors in this market are nice to deal with. I have consistently found them to be real and helpful people. They are always ready to help, as far as their time permits, a beginner who is really trying. They reject material by letter when it is humanly possible – not by the inhuman rejection slip.' The passage concludes with an exhortation to the writer always to ask for more money if he thinks he is worth it, something which Alexander never failed to do.

In one sense Alexander was part of the old world. The tone of much of his advice is saturated with the Protestant work ethic sufficient to gladden the heart of any ironmaster or Primitive Methodist preacher. The writer had improved himself by his own hard work and it is not difficult to detect a note of lofty disdain in his work for those lacking the same degree of application. It is worth pointing out again that democratic though the new face of British politics might be, and against the background of a general passion for classlessness,

Shrewsbury, *c.*1946: 'If Rosina needed a new coat I just wrote another short story.'

Alexander was more than happy to use his army rank and to place his heroes and heroines firmly among the middle class.

For several years after the war people had been content to seek a return to pre-war values and what they saw as that period's certainties but now, with Anthony Eden's Conservative administration newly in power, a more hard-edged type of society, less rooted in tradition and patriotism but with its consumerist edge much more finely honed, was serving notice that it would, in its own good time, come to dominate

British life. The package which was to shake Alexander out of his post-war cosiness and to launch him headlong into the world of the professional author was indistinguishable from the other packages, envelopes and packets casually dropped off the train at Abergavenny station, sorted, then bundled off in the van to the little post office at Llanellen. The galley proofs of *A Thought of Honour* sent by the Museum Press (now defunct) for him to correct and return must have given him the first taste of being an author rather than a mere wordsmith beating out stories for the women's market. There were his words, hastily pulled and roughly printed on long strips of paper, but his nevertheless. They were words which had somehow fought their way through a forest of rivals to catch the eye of a commissioning editor. A few weeks later, after the proofs had been corrected and returned, a cheque for £75 made out in his name arrived in the post. In those days £75, whilst not a princely sum, could buy a decent second-hand car and settle the household bills of all but the most improvident. The money was an advance on sales and he might have harboured expectations of more to follow. In fact the book only just broke even. Throughout his life Alexander would say that his first adventure in novel-writing had ended in disappointment but he was making a comparison between *A Thought of Honour*, his apprentice piece, and the books from his most productive and profitable period, not altogether a fair comparison. He was lucky to have fought his way through to publication, and he knew it. A good-sized cheque, although it may have looked meagre in comparison with the royalties of much later, was safely in the bank.

With the publication of *A Thought of Honour* George Alexander Graber, already known by some people in and around Abergavenny as something of a writer, could hold his head up high and greet people in the pub and the workplace with an easy acceptance of the admiration which was his due. He was on his way. To use an expression which he borrowed from Chinese sources, the longest journey begins with a single step. It was a firm and determined foot which took the first step to literary fame and fortune. No matter to Alexander Graber that *A Thought of Honour*, when it appeared in 1954, did not carry all before it in literary terms or in the amount of remuneration he was to receive. He had broken into the charmed circle.

It was after the book's acceptance by Museum Press that Alexander adopted the name by which he was to be popularly known for the rest of his life. It came about after a call from the publishers, the editor on the other end somewhat hesitantly suggesting a change of name on the grounds that Graber sounded too Germanic. 'Rosina came up with the solution,' he later said. 'We had both admired the American politician Cordell Hull and thought his first name rather unusual. Rosina said I should drop the "George" and make "Alexander" my first name and "Cordell" the last name. Put together, "Alexander" and "Cordell" had the right rhythm and feel to them.' Indeed they had. Alexander was pleased by the way Cordell at once gave the impression of being the name of a rakish hero and of suggesting tough, sinewy strength. With his own good looks and undoubted determination the name was suited to the man. So successful was the pseudonym that few people called him anything else.

Alexander admitted that *A Thought of Honour* was autobiographical. As an assertion it is largely true. On page 61 of the edition published by White Lion in 1973, Alexander's character Tietjens reminisces how at the onset of the First World War his old mother had flung her arms around him and tearfully warned him not to sleep between damp sheets, the exact words Alexander ascribed to his own grandmother before their final parting. The novel centres on the lives of the men who designed and tested 'Funnies' during the war, the women who loved them and the brass hats of the War Office who imposed suicidal demands upon the soldiers. The novel opens in Africa, a continent of which Alexander knew almost nothing. Still, the opening chapter is evocative. A steamer is making its lazy way down a muddy tropical river. There are two white men aboard, Walter Tietjens, the manager of a trading post, and John Macmasters.

Tietjens is a ruthlessly ambitious little man who has already been cuckolded once and is to be so again by Macmasters. In his spare time and at his own expense, Tietjens is designing and building some sort of military landing-barge. Earlier in the war, of course, Alexander had been involved with barge construction. It is quite possible that the name Tietjens is taken from somebody of Flemish or Dutch origin whom he came to know at that time.

A Thought of Honour has a compelling plot and credible characters and has a fine sense of time and place. Alexander takes the reader into the threadbare pubs and hotels and builds in the mind's eye a picture of a desolate stretch of coast, the Suffolk coast he knew at first hand. The men, working long hours at dangerous work, are stretched to the point at which they might snap and the very countryside seems exhausted and sick of war. Despite the wealth of military detail, which is obviously culled from the author's own experience, it is an anti-war book. Alexander was telling the truth when, many years later, he said that he had written it in order to 'try and get the war out of my system'. Whether he did so successfully is another matter. To the very end of his life Alexander would talk about his war experiences without bitterness, and even with a certain amount of nostalgia.

Despite what the author was to say of it, *A Thought of Honour* was by any standards a more than competent book even if the military detail occasionally veered towards the irksome. In it we see some of the curious little literary curlicues which were to make Alexander Cordell's style distinctive. For instance, where a less individualistic writer might say a warning flag was 'snapping in the gale' he says simply that the flag is 'for gale'. This goes further than merely describing a warning flag stiffened by the wind by implying some sort of complicity in the weather on the part of the flag.

Although Alexander was to dismiss *A Thought of Honour* as an apprentice piece, many readers think it the equal of some of his later work. Certainly for those interested in the author's personality, many of his attitudes are here laid bare. Immersed in male culture since his childhood days, Alexander valued the friendship of men, which he expressed in a way which to some might nowadays seem rather dated, belonging to the world of John Buchan rather than that of contemporary sexual politics. One such passage opines that 'Women rant like Hell about loyalty' but rarely show any. The love of one man for another, on the other hand, is something to be cherished as a rare jewel. It asks for nothing in recompense and needs no physical contact to bolster its sincerity. It exists unspoken, unattached to cheap romantic situations, and is unswerving to the brink of death. 'When the chap next to you will pull you off the wire without a thought of death, that is the final test of love. It's the whole emotion in its purest form.' These words were written in 1953 and the view expressed in them never changed. For the rest of his life Alexander would say approvingly of a man: 'He's the sort of chap who would pull you off the wire.' For a writer who was to cut his teeth on what in those days was called 'the feminine market' and whose female characters, like Morfydd in *Rape of the Fair Country*, were to have more than their fair share of masculine virtues, these are perhaps strange sentiments. Although Alexander did indeed make much more of his women characters in later books, the loyalty which men were capable of showing one another was a constant theme. Indeed, it was one of the underpinnings of his own life.

One curious point in *A Thought of Honour* is that a Major O'Neil is referred to as 'Sam', by which name Alexander says he was called by at least one superior officer during his Orford Ness days. Generally, though, the author identifies with Macmasters. It is usually not wise to over-identify characters with their creators but Macmasters and the female character Loetia share several traits with Alexander and Rosina who, in 1946, had looked forward to a time in which they could finally be together and claim their share of the post-war dream.

Throughout his life Alexander always read the reviews of his books and one in particular on the publication of *A Thought of Honour* touched a nerve. The *Herald of Wales*, published in Swansea, wrote, 'Perhaps Mr Cordell will be able to write a novel about Wales, its legends, its customs and its people. It should be worth the effort.' It was a casual remark on the part of the journalist. Alexander's connections with Wales were slight enough and his next work could have taken any direction. Books about the war were still achieving more than respectable sales and he might have considered this a vein still to be worth quarrying. But the walks around the Blorenge, talking with local people and inspecting the ruins from over a century before had done their work. They prompted him to write about Wales, but it was a different Wales from the one that the *Herald*, with its implications of pixies and fairies and tales from the Mabinogion, had in mind. It was to be a tough thing, torn from the living sinews of the land and rooted in experience that still hovered on the edge of the Welsh consciousness.

Throughout 1954 and into the next year the sales of *A Thought of Honour* remained lacklustre and in fact were only ever to cover the advance. The next book would leave it standing within days of publication. There was as yet no name for it, no theme, no characters and no plot, although there was a location and a period. But it was a potent idea. In the early days of its coalescing Alexander would take the elements of its construction as they came to him, mull them over during walks, or in slack periods at work and build them into the barely discernible framework that was nevertheless taking shape in his mind like some grand seagoing vessel being assembled on its stocks. It did not even have a name, but one was to come in the strangest way that any story-teller had the right to expect.

Chapter Seven

On the day in that late summer of 1957 with which this book opens, after he had inspected what remained of the old Blorenge tramroad, Alexander remounted his autocycle and continued up the mountain, past the point where the trees gave out, and there met an old man. The two exchanged greetings. Desolate is the adjective most commonly used to describe the Blorenge's northern flank where the village of Garndyrus crouched precariously above the slope called the Tumble with the dark valley below. In winter the place comes to resemble tundra but in summer the chasing clouds cause patterns of light to run across the valley and, bald though the mountain top may be, its severity is soon relieved for the traveller by the beeches which crowd the Blorenge's flanks. It is only when looking to the south-west in the direction of Blaenavon that the viewer sees plainly the extent to which the land has been ripped and scarred. It was in this direction Alexander was looking when he remarked that the land must have been terribly exploited by the industrial revolution. 'Exploited, mun? This country has been raped!' the old man said, and the spark ignited Alexander's imagination. It seemed to him that the land which had provided the iron which gave Garndyrus its short butterfly-day of life had now yielded to him a precious gift: *Rape of the Fair Country*. Pleased to have a receptive audience, the old man promised to tell Alexander more of the area's history. They agreed to meet the following evening at the Rolling Mill pub in Broad Street, Blaenavon. Avid for what he sensed might be material, Alexander mounted his autocycle the next night and laboured up the mountain and into Blaenavon, dismounting and entering to see several old colliers but not the one he sought. He bought himself a drink and smiled at the other men but sat some distance from them. After a while, the men invited him into their company and he told them why he had come to the inn.

'I think the old gentleman I planned to meet was going to introduce me to you,' he said.

'You've not heard then?' one of the men asked. 'He died last night.' It occurred to Alexander that he may have been the last human being to whom the old man ever spoke and that his very last words had afforded the title of the book he was to write.

When it eventually appeared on 12 January 1959, *Rape of the Fair Country* was reviewed alongside some of the finest books of the day. Literary lions like J. B. Priestley praised it and in newspapers and magazines across the English-speaking world the adjective mills were working overtime. 'Lusty', 'splendid', 'wild, full of lyrical beauty' were run-of-the-mill praises. Other reviewers called it 'bubbling with the juices of life' (the *Washington Post*) and 'sonorous, with a Bible-like beauty'. Aneurin Bevan, the towering figure of the British Left and MP for Ebbw Vale, was quoted in the American papers as saying the book was 'tremendous'. Gratifying though it must have been to be reviewed in the *Roanoke Times*, the *Albany Orc – Democrat Herald* and the *Columbus Dispatch*, Alexander could hardly have been more pleased by the reviews he was getting in the British papers. The American reviews were long and discursive and tended to regurgitate the plots and sprinkle a few adjectives around the article. Their British counterparts were bright and punchy and aimed at the popular audience it was necessary to reach if commercial success was to keep pace with the critical acclaim. In the *Empire News* and *Sunday Chronicle* Gareth Bowen, a Welshman, went the full hog under the screaming headline 'Brilliant, Bawdy – It's a Knockout!' The text is equally breathless. 'Today I introduce an incredible novel about Wales . . . a sexy, sizzling saga which is about to hit the literary world sideways. It's got "truth" blazoned on every page . . . and it's written by an Englishman,' Bowen effused, the implication of the last few words being that Englishmen do not normally write the truth about Wales. Bowen, or rather the sub-editors who handled his copy, split the story up into three sections each with its own cross-heading – 'love', 'life' and 'labour'. Under 'love' Bowen picks out the passage: 'Trembling are the fingers that twist and seek, searching . . . blindly in the darkness.' Under 'life' he cites: 'A day I want to remember, this one. A bloody nose, a tooth in one hand and another in Dada's pocket and a boot in the belly.' Under 'labour' was given a description of the amount of work Alexander had put into the book. In Bowen's eyes he had become a hero along with his own characters. Alexander is reported as saying, 'The book is 100,000 words long but I wrote about half a million before I got what I wanted. I spent hours researching at the National Library of Wales at Aberystwyth and at Newport Public Library.' The comment is at odds with his usual claim that the book was dashed off quickly, at white heat. Alexander apparently thought that such an admission might not look good in the press and decided to paint the picture of a more painstaking writer.

Almost from the start, he knew the value of publicity and usually knew the right things to say to the press. In return for the acres of favourable coverage he received over the years, he was unfailingly generous to journalists, never hesitating to speak to the smallest or most obscure publication or the most unpractised of interviewers. Part of this was an instinctive feeling that having started on the very lowest slopes of literary endeavour himself, he should never scorn the base degrees through which he had ascended. He would happily admit, though, that all publicity was welcome, provided of course, it was of the right kind. Alexander Cordell could be very prickly about adverse criticism. The breezy comment in the *Empire News* that he had worked through half-a-million words before finishing *Rape of the Fair Country* is exaggeration, pure and simple, a prime example of Alexander wishing to make himself appear the struggling and dedicated artist. Ever since arriving at Llanellen, Alexander had begun to enter writing competitions, mostly importantly one organized by the *South Wales Argus*, the local evening newspaper. Writing was not, in its early stages, a matter of inspiration. As a practical, working writer, Alexander knew that anyone who sat behind his desk waiting for inspiration to come might be waiting for months. 'Writing is one part inspiration, nine parts perspiration' was the old saw he often quoted. His work was conducted on a professional basis, without affectation. Professional soldiers have a saying, 'Time spent on reconnaissance is rarely wasted'. As a soldier and also an engineer who knew that one must organize and prepare one's materials before construction can begin, Alexander did his 'reconnaissance' work thoroughly.

Not that it was all work during those years. In those days only the relatively well-off could afford foreign travel. For most working-class people the summer holiday was simply a matter of getting on a train and disembarking at the local resort for a week or a fortnight of dancing, beer-drinking, 'housey-housey' as bingo was then called, and wet afternoons spent in penny amusement arcades. The Grabers, Joneses and Tribbles were in the more fortunate position of being able to take long summer holidays which allowed them to range all over the countryside.

For these families, west Wales is the most obvious holiday venue, the land of mountain and coastline on their doorsteps. Tom Jones, Alexander's wartime friend, was an Oswestry boy and for many years before the war had gone on holiday with his parents to Borth, a coastal village a few miles to the north of Aberystwyth where his family would stay in a cottage near the railway station.

In fact it was not to Borth but to Llandudno that the Grabers and the Joneses and their respective children, Georgina and Julie, went for their first family holiday together. Peggy Jones recalls that a man who had served with her and Rosina in the Observer Corps had bought a hotel in the resort. It may have been that the children did not like the inevitable restraints of hotel life or that, even with the reduction in prices made especially for friends, it was still too expensive, but for future holidays their attention turned to Borth, a place which Alexander had discovered during the war while recuperating at Harlech.

The seaside village is a curve of houses and shops, clinging to the rim of a shingled beach. Victorian houses mingle with much older, simpler, whitewashed Welsh houses clustered in the middle of the village with more modern angular and balconied buildings situated to the north. It was on the southern arm of the thinning crescent of population which meets a headland to the south where the Grabers, Joneses and sometimes the Tribbles rented a holiday cottage.

Alexander, Rosina and Georgina journeyed up from the south. The Joneses had a little car in which adults, children and luggage would be wedged for a journey of some eighty miles across the Welsh mountains to the sea. A photograph evidently taken by Georgina, then aged nine or ten, has the authentic salty smack of those seaside holidays. Tom, his thinning hair plastered across his forehead and wearing enormous hand-knitted swimming trunks, is holding a towel with his wife Peggy, wearing one of the inelegant rubber bathing caps which were thought necessary in those days, in the centre, and a shivering Mary in front of her. Alexander, slightly taller than Tom, has a bronzed face but apart from bathing seems to have been disinclined to undress, for his body is still pallid. Other pictures show Alexander with Peggy and Phyllis and children with Alexander clad in shirt, pullover and jacket, although a concession to the summer heat is the removal of his tie.

For the children the least enjoyable part of these holidays would be being bundled into cars or trains bound for Borth. For Alexander, though, the journey was one of increasing anticipation, not only of the obvious pleasures of a family holiday but also of the reunion with a landscape that had become a part of his creative imagination.

Nowadays, summer trippers pour onto the sands of the Dyfi estuary on the Borth side, but in those days, when there were far fewer vehicles and people took their pleasures less intrusively, it was possible even at the height of summer to look upon the scene with Cader Idris and the rearing height of Snowdon to the north and imagine that the scene must have had a more than passing resemblance to the Creation.

During the book's incubation Alexander's little family had been living at Llanellen but by the time of its construction he had moved to 7 Holywell Crescent in nearby Abergavenny. In 1959 the war was only fourteen years away and still impressed on Alexander's memory. One of

Summer holidays: at Borth in the late 1950s, with (left to right) Julie Jones, mother Margaret Jones, Rosina and Georgina.

the first things he did after moving into the new home was to have the name 'Ubique' displayed outside. The word is part of the motto of the Corps of Royal Engineers and means 'Everywhere'. To his public Alexander was now Alexander Cordell, the local writer. To himself, he was Major George Alexander Graber, Royal Engineers, no fey intellectual or pansified versifier but the tough, retired professional soldier, the Hemingway end of the market rather than the Gore Vidal. The move to Ubique, on the southern outskirts of Abergavenny was made so that Georgina could be nearer her school and Alexander his work. Nowadays the move would be seen as an odd one. The new home was, while pleasant, nondescript, one of many dozens that had sprung up to house the town's managerial class, the middle-ranking railway officials, civil servants and shopkeepers. The Lodge at Llanellen, although today virtually unchanged since Alexander lived there, is a highly desirable and distinctive country home, tucked under a fold in the hills and away from the hurly-burly of the town. Even the immense increase in the amount of traffic between Abergavenny and the string of towns to the south has hardly impinged upon its seclusion. In the 1950s, though, while it was the sort of isolated, self-contained little country dwelling that might have appealed to one of Alexander's craggy-jawed heroes or individualistic heroines, The Lodge was not the ideal place to bring up a young family. Getting up, making breakfast and checking through what he had written the night before meant an early and also a cold start. Time spent travelling was time not spent writing. With the scent of success in his nostrils, even if the tangible results of it were not yet in the bank, Alexander was beginning to resent anything that kept him away from his desk. The small depot where he went daily to work was only a few hundred yards from his new home. Anyone who can remember these years will recall the slumbrousness of them, the desire and instinct to find the sort of peace and contentment which people imagined had reigned before the war, even though such a peace had never existed in any country or time, outside their own imaginations. Long before the days of modern management techniques and widespread privatization and the bottom-line accounting of not only profits but also work time, work was generally less arduous, even if hours were longer. This applied nowhere more than the civil service where the feeling still persisted that education and rank were themselves sufficient to earn some ease at work. It is not surprising under the circumstances that Alexander was not to quit full-time employment until the late 1960s, almost ten years after the publication of *Rape of the Fair Country* had made him famous.

The job was boring but otherwise perfect. Even in the lunch-hour it was a relatively easy matter to get to the library in Abergavenny, in the Victorian building which still houses the library today. For Rosina, too, the new location was more amenable than the cold and remote Lodge at Llanellen. Abergavenny is a prosperous little town, its market bursting with fruit and vegetables, books and knick-knacks, all purveyed under the soaring roof of the old Market Hall which gives the place something of the feeling of a bazaar. In the market all sorts of goods may have been on sale from moleskin trousers for farmers to parts for ex-army lorries and tools and local produce, fine eggs and creamy milk, but for Alexander the greatest treasure of all was the speech of the townspeople. His own speech and that of Rosina, and that of most of his friends in Shrewsbury, had been standard received English. Now he was able to hear all around him the more musical cadences of the Welsh. True, being within a few miles of the English border this was not the sing-song of north or west Wales but there was a lilt which the Englishman found exciting and a little baffling. 'I would often hang around the market, just listening to the way the women spoke,' Alexander would say, particularly when questioned as to how he hit on the knack of inverting sentences spoken by his characters to give them a Welsh flavour.

At Ubique, 1960.

Living in Abergavenny also meant a more active social life, even for Alexander who was prone to bouts of reclusiveness. When the family moved into Holywell Crescent, Max Donovan and his wife, Elsie May, were already living at number 5 and a lively friendship ensued. Miss Dorothy Watkins lived with the Donovans as a lodger for some years and retains a clear recollection of those days which were to prove the fulcrum upon which the rest of Alexander's life was to balance.

Max was the manager of the Home and Colonial stores opposite Burtons in Abergavenny. He was a very smart man but at that time in poor health. One day Elsie was going to see her sister in Bournemouth but Max wasn't feeling very well and, as he often did, lay on the floor in front of the fire. Alex took Elsie to Newport station and as he drove asked her if she thought her husband would be all right. 'Yes,' she said. After that he would say, 'Actually, I fancied her then, but she was always Mrs Donovan to me.' He came back to Rosina and said Max wasn't very well and Rosina said Elsie shouldn't have gone. It wasn't very long afterwards that Max died. Alex used to say that he liked Elsie.

What attention Alexander was not lavishing upon his family was being spent on his writing career. He had already been collating the results of his explorations in the Blaenavon area at the time of the announcement in the *South Wales Argus* of a prize for the most interesting literary project. Never a man to waste any effort, he began to collect into a submission for the prize the snatches of dialogue and historical fact which he had already garnered for the book that was to be *Rape of the Fair Country*.

The sixty-three-page workbook of which he submitted a copy to the *Argus* is an extraordinary document in that it serves virtually as a manifesto of the author's intentions. *A Thought of Honour* was autobiographical with elements of plot thrown in. In its very early stages it would have looked to the casual observer that *Rape of the Fair Country* might be a local history rather than a novel. The technique Alexander was to use for the rest of his life is laid out in a little section entitled 'Research' right at the end of the submission:

To many publications and documents the writer is indebted for the facts contained herein, but to none in particular. No single document lays down in detail the social history, during the period selected, of the people of Garndyrus and Blaenavon. That was why this paper was attempted. The period, being beyond the reach of living memory, could be reached only through the elderly, the men whose pride lies in Garndyrus and Blaenavon, and whose recollection of 'handed down' facts proved extremely clear. Upon word of mouth therefore, and private help, is this paper based, rather than upon recognized authority. No apology is offered for its 'reconstruction' method of telling, since it was the only vehicle available.

The submission was entitled 'Life among the Ironworkers of Garndyrus and Blaenavon 1810 to 1836'; the frontispiece is in a decorative script by the author, its contents touching upon the social and industrial history of the towns together with copious notes and photographs. In the foreword dated July 1957, Alexander spells out the fact that the writing of *Rape of the Fair Country* had commenced. Extracts shown in quotation marks, he warned the reader, were snatches of dialogue from the novel in hand and were therefore the fictional words of the characters. 'It is hoped that readers are not deterred by this form of presentation which, the writer believes, is made no less factual by its invention, but perhaps brings to a history a needed, more personal note,' he pleads. The prologue begins with the unnamed character, obviously Iestyn Mortymer, walking over the mountain by night 'into the furnace glare where the drop-hammers were thumping'. Although the text appears in inverted commas the words do not constitute the opening of *Rape of the Fair Country*. Compared with what is to come, this is workaday stuff but he obviously liked the imagery of the 'drop-hammers thumping' for it does indeed make an appearance within the first few paragraphs of the novel. As the father and son walk over the mountain – presumably from Blaenavon, the Mortymers' home – to Garndyrus, the ore-carriers with their long barrows that could carry half a ton, the ostlers with their pack-mules bringing limestone from the Tumble quarries, the colliers running the coal trams from Pwlldu, the children of only seven years staggering under various loads and the old men and women straining out the last of their lives in brutal labour, are all paraded past the reader. As part of the background, smoke and steam are billowing, red and hellish in the glare and all the time the iron pinks and clanks 'under a hundred hammers'.

Having regarded with some misgiving that which is to be his workplace, Iestyn is taken into the Garndyrus Inn where Billy Harri, the landlord, is sitting in the window mending the banners for the Benefit (the co-operative organization which prefigures the trade union), a somewhat unlikely activity in view of the fact that the public house is already crowded out by night-shift workers who were 'paying back their sweat in beer'. Dada warns Iestyn, 'Never let me see you in here, for drink is the downfall of good men and starvation for their wives and children,' which is an odd thing to say since they are already in the pub. Still, it is at the Garndyrus Inn that Iestyn is signed up for the iron trade at the rate of sixpence a day. Not much, but as Iestyn reflects, 'Better than Abergavenny Hiring Fair at which one may be hired out virtually as a chattel to any landlord who cares to make a bid: for a boy never knew what owner he would land with, and some of them were devils with the stick.'

Some Marxists, though approving of the general tenor of Alexander's work, were to claim that he had failed to display sufficient 'class consciousness' in *Rape of the Fair Country*. Alexander, though, instinctively understood that real life is not, and never was, so mechanistic. Very rich men could do good things and very poor ones could do evil. It is certainly true that the ironmasters were brashly and unashamedly rich and sometimes appeared callous, but it is also true that they were themselves of lowly origins. It was not the aristocratic Marquis of Abergavenny that leased the land upon which Garndyrus and Blaenavon stood who turned it into the crucible of the Industrial Revolution. It was three sometime proletarians with the distinctly unaristocratic names of Hopkins, Hill and Pratt who literally forged a new social order. The wonder is that, having for so many years been encouraged to view society through the conventional and conservative prism of the Army, Alexander had drawn his own conclusions which led him incontrovertibly into the left-wing camp. It may well be that the Alexander Cordell of 1997 would not have agreed with the Alexander Cordell of 1957 who described the terrifying Scotch Cattle thus: 'Men who took secret oaths and banded together to force the rest of the community to their will . . . the leader of such a band was called The Bull. Selected for his strength and cruelty, he dressed himself in skins and adorned himself with the horns of a bull or cow.' Upon this description of an almost shamanistic leader is grafted a description of his methods, and those of the band which he led. The house of a blackleg was daubed with a sign of a bull's head prior to attack. Retribution would come, although the terrified inhabitants would not know precisely when. When the Scotch Cattle struck, the house was ransacked, the furniture burned and the husband flogged. They sometimes purposely broke limbs and there was the occasional murder.

Whatever the shortcomings of the Scotch Cattle in terms of their class perspectives, their role in keeping Alexander's story-line cracking along is beyond doubt. The confrontation between Dai Probert, leader of the Scotch Cattle, and other residents of the two towns so brilliantly described in *Rape of the Fair Country* has its origins in the competition submission already mentioned. Alexander relished the fight scene which is almost cinematic. Mr Afel Hughes takes off his spectacles – 'always a sign of trouble' – as Dic Shon Ffyrnig slips little bands of iron over his knuckles. Will Blaenavon, pugilist, was climbing over the counter, 'looking as happy as sin with his barrel-tapper in his fist . . . If the ancient Welsh had fought the Romans as we fought the Cattle that night the devils would never have built Caerleon'. Although Iestyn acquits himself well in this fight, he is chastised when his father gets to hear of the rumpus. Greatly though Dada hates the Scotch Cattle and pleased though he might be to see them get a thrashing, Iestyn has broken the cardinal rule – he had consumed strong liquor – and for Dada, who was a deacon, that was everything.

Alexander always said (except to reporters) that *Rape of the Fair Country* was written at white heat with the pages pouring from his typewriter with little thought as to plot or composition. Its very ebullience shows it to be a book that was written, not merely constructed. Vivid colours and action are everywhere as in the description of the annual Benefit Night led by Billy Harri, the landlord of the Garndyrus Inn who has the colours of the club tied round his waist and on a stick and is flanked by torch-bearers. Dafydd Cut-in-Half follows behind on a little trolley pulled by Tall Jim and Owen and Griff Howells are blasting away on their trombones. Mr Gwallter has the bass drum on his stomach, 'hitting it for holes', and Will Blaenavon, the pugilist, is going hard on the horn. Piccolos, flutes, cymbals and whistles flare and thump their way into the story and even Enid the Donkey is in the parade with beer barrels hanging on either side and Phil Benjamin hanging on her tail. Contrast is what makes the passage work as well as the subliminal hints at a pagan procession. The parade is at night, and in the mind's eye the torches are flaring off the brass instruments. Given that none of the men are professional musicians and their instruments may be old and battered and, presumably, often pawned, one imagines a rather flat marching sound. The presence of Dafydd Cut-in-Half reminds us that death and mutilation in the forges and mines were never far from Alexander's mind but he is dramatically contrasted by Tall Jim towing his trolley. Enid the Donkey, with her beer barrels strapped on her back, sounds a note of religious ritual but also, perhaps, something darker, deeper and more ancient. Shades of society within the working classes are beautifully observed and drawn. As the iron towns grow, rowdy and profane men flood in, bringing with them bull-baiting and cock-fighting and bloody combats with bare fists. Counterpointing this, chapels are built and become full of pious people who see the current afflictions of the Welsh as a time of trial which must be endured if they are to emerge into the full glory of God's light. Next to a terrible scene of a bullfight in which a bull-terrier is hanging from the tormented animal's nose with the blood-maddened owner screaming encouragement, Alexander describes Welsh homes with their tiny windows prim with lace curtains and snug against winter gales and blizzards within which a deeply rooted religious faith abides. Little nuggets of information are scattered throughout *Rape of the Fair Country*, the result of Alexander's gleanings in libraries and talking to old local people. When there was a fight between Dada and Rhys Jenkins with Jenkins, all six feet five and seventeen stones of him coming off the worst, Iestyn's mother makes off to Jenkins's house to bandage him, 'which is the strangest custom the English have ever heard of, they say, but the way in Garndyrus of making friends out of enemies. And Rhys Jenkins, after that Sunday, was our friend for life.'

All his life Alexander had a great regard for local historians, the men and women who publish papers or slim volumes on some aspect of local lore and are then quickly forgotten; the mayflies of the literary and academic worlds. One such work which attracted local attention at the time Alexander was conducting his researches in the 1950s was an essay entitled 'Blaenavon and Iron' by Eddie Davies, written for the first meeting of the Blaenavon Local History Society. It was undoubtedly one of the pieces of published research which added fuel to Alexander's creative furnaces. He not only read everything available about the life of the ironworkers but walked the ground and even indulged in rudimentary archaeology. He describes the ruins of the winch house which is part of the gravity-operated tramroad running from Llanfoist up the flanks of the Blorenge and even speculates, from what remained in 1957, as to the size of the Garndyrus furnaces. One evening in the late 1980s while walking with Richard Frame near the Lamb and Fox at Pwlldu, Alexander stopped and pointed across the valley to the low mounds and ridges which were all that were left of Garndyrus, picked out by the rays of the setting sun.

'From this point I scoured the area with binoculars before crossing the valley and pacing out the dimensions,' he said. His training as a surveyor had been put to the service of literature. In an interview published in the *East Anglian Daily Times* on 12 January 1959, Alexander spoke more about his reconnoitring of the Welsh countryside and of his chosen mount. He had walked hundreds of miles, he said: 'I also used an autocycle which I purchased second-hand for £10. It carried me two thousand miles through those rugged hills in all weathers. When it got too hot I often packed snow around the engine to cool it, or scooped water from mountain streams.' In fact, Alexander left very little to chance when it came to research. The back part of his submission to the *South Wales Argus* contains precisely drawn maps and photographs. Much of this detailed information was gleaned from visits to the National Library of Wales and from friendly librarians in Abergavenny, Cardiff and Newport. Throughout his life Alexander was generous in his praise of the men and women whose diligence provides much of the raw data from which historical novelists work. Government reports from the period under consideration provided much of the information he required, but to use his own term, this would have remained 'as dry as dust' history were it not moulded into powerful fiction by the force of his own imagination.

In short, the man who wrote 'Life among the Ironworkers of Garndyrus and Blaenavon' was perfectly primed to write a powerful historical novel. In the June of 1957, by which time the submission was complete, all the building blocks were in place. The writer endowed with more than the average amount of diligence also had a background in engineering which made it easy for him to grasp the technical aspects of iron-working and the machinery associated with it. His writing style and capacity for constructing a plot and sustaining a story had been tested in the women's market and he had sufficient free time to pursue his researches with the incalculable benefit of a supportive wife.

Chapter Eight

Rape of the Fair Country was written virtually without pause, the author working into the small hours and putting aside social commitments until the book ended with the Chartists singing their anthem on the way to transportation and the two little words that every writer delights to type: The End.

'I had turned into an anti-social animal during the writing but the book had to come before everything,' he would say. 'I worked all through the hours when decent men and women were in their beds and only disreputables like me were abroad. I never doubted that the book under my hand would be published. The story was crying out to be told. It demanded to be told.'

One morning, Alexander put the cover over his Remington, carefully squared the pile of manuscript and put it in a brown paper parcel with a covering note and, on his way to work, dropped it at the post office in Abergavenny. Executives at Victor Gollancz had already seen sample chapters and knew what to expect. *Rape of the Fair Country* perfectly fitted the left-wing leanings of the publishing firm, yet had the action and love interest that appealed to a popular audience. Several nail-biting weeks elapsed before Gollancz wrote back to the author to say that the editorial board's decision had been to submit the book to two readers who would then report on its likelihood of commercial success. Joy was unrestrained when a letter from Gollancz dropped onto the mat at Holywell Crescent to be snatched up and ripped open with, as Alexander recalls it, trembling fingers.

I leaned up against the wall hardly reading the actual words, just gleaning the sense that my book had been accepted. Rosina had come into the passage. I looked at her and shouted, 'This is it! I think we've done it this time!' It was some time before we came back down to earth. It had happened with *A Thought of Honour* to some extent, but in my water I knew this was it.

Even by the standards of the day when potential best-sellers were hyped to a much wider extent, the treatment the book received upon publication was superb. Daily newspapers selling to communities of a few thousand townsfolk and scattered American prairie farmers were, by the early months of 1959, carrying syndicated reviews on *Rape of the Fair Country*, a story set in hilly, damp land wreathed with Celtic ghosts and shades of a past which it was impossible for most of them to reconstruct from the details of their own daily lives. Gollancz had carefully primed literary and left-wing figures – Aneurin Bevan, the Tredegar boy who was architect of the National Health Service, the actor and playwright Emlyn Williams and novelists Gwyn Thomas and Jack Jones – to sing the praises of Alexander's book. No less a figure than J. B. Priestley joined in the general chorus of approbation. In *Reynold's News* of 11 January 1959 Priestley's praise roared and soared:

> A tremendous book, an exciting book – and so on and so forth, boy! We can almost hear Welsh harps and hymns . . . This is all to the good. It will do no harm to raise the temperature of book-publishing, book-selling and book-buying, especially if the novel in question belongs to literature and not to the over-cropped field of war memoirs. Let us by all means make a noise about a few authors instead of firing 20-gun salutes to field-marshals.

Such a review in a then-renowned although now defunct magazine pleased Alexander mightily as well as confirming his view that while one war novel had been a sort of purgative, he had been wise not to follow along the well-trodden path of war books. J. B. Priestley did quibble about some aspects of the book, suggesting at one point in the lengthy review that men and women who spent most of their waking hours in back-breaking labour would not have the energy to sing, dance and fight. He concludes, however, that the author may be allowed his poetic licence. Priestley compliments Alexander on being 'reasonably accurate' in terms of his historical research before himself going on to place the action in Brecon, which is many miles to the north. Still, these were quibbles, things that must be said to point up the laudatory nature of the review. The article of over a thousand words ended, 'Finally, I hope that Alexander Cordell – and it is a name new to me – soon enjoys the success he well deserves. To all readers except those who have been running away from life so long they cannot stop, I recommend most warmly and gratefully *Rape of the Fair Country*.'

Alexander must have been delighted with the remarks in publicity material contributed by Aneurin Bevan who had been given a review copy.

> It is a tremendous book; an exciting book. There is not a single dull or jaded character and the story moves from incident to incident without faltering. There is a passion and a pity rarely to be found in novels of

historical evocation. The events Alexander Cordell writes about are sufficiently near in time and for me at any rate, familiar in their setting, to carry a haunting sense of authenticity.

If that sounded just a little too much like a publicist's blurb, Gwyn Thomas was there to provide a more literary note. 'It's a real shaker, a most remarkable bit of compassionate evocation. Knowing the places, the people, the sounds, it struck deep into me. For all the terror of which it tells there is a sheen of laughing goodness over it; a quick, lyrical humour silvers even the savagery of it.'

With such thundering endorsements from the elder statesmen of literature and the Left, a perhaps more objective view in the *Oxford Mail* would not have troubled the author, for in those days Brian Aldiss had not achieved eminence as a science fiction writer and critic.

It's the sort of thing a lesser publisher might have described as 'lusty', 'gutsy', 'busty' and 'bawdy': instead Mr Gollancz gives us a leaflet of praise from Aneurin Bevan, Gwyn Thomas, etc. True, the novel's characters are big and vigorous and the style is rococo Welsh-English . . . there are many earthy scenes – the mating of pigs and of humans – and with the Unions and the Chartists in the background the whole has a historical power. But its model is too obviously those big American sagas about the Good Bad Old Days. Even its title must have been chosen with one eye on Vistavision.

No less a Welsh figure than Goronwy Rees, writing in the *Listener*, struck pretty much the same note:

Rape of the Fair Country disappoints only because we feel cheated by the preliminary fanfare of publicity and Mr Aneurin Bevan's solemn assurance that this is a 'tremendous book'. To this, Mr Jack Jones, Mr Gwyn Thomas and Mr Emlyn Williams add their chorus of praise . . . Perhaps one should not be surprised to discover, after all this, that *Rape of the Fair Country* is simply a historical novel of the straightforward best-selling variety, full of tempestuous passions, lusty adventurers, beautiful and promiscuous ladies and the naked opposition of virtue and vice, the only difference being that the glamour and kitsch which are usually devoted to the service of wealth are here lavished upon the poor.

Goronwy Rees goes on, not without a certain amount of humour, to suggest that the book sometimes comes across as a *Gone with the Wind* of the Welsh valleys, but he does temper his snootiness by admitting that description and research are excellent. He concludes that the novel, for all its violence to which he objects 'is excellent. What a pity he should have chosen to embellish it with boyish, long-legged narrow-hipped women with false poetry and a kind of proletarian glamour which is no less offensive than the more glossy kind.'

Readers of *The Times* were informed three days after publication that Alexander had 'force' and 'creative impulse' and that the book was 'full-blooded . . . even though the reader might feel at times that here and there the colours have been laid on a bit too thick'. In general terms the intellectual end of the market admired the force of Alexander's prose and the craftsmanship of his plot while remaining sniffy about what it saw as an excess of adjectival colour. The popular and middle-market press was unstinting in its praise. At any rate, the sheaves of favourable review clippings collected by Durrant's press cuttings service and forwarded to the author far outweighed those of reviewers whom *Rape of the Fair Country* had failed to impress. As any author with pretensions to writing a best-seller knows, a good review in a mid-market newspaper counteracts ten sniping ones in the highbrow journals. As for the proletarian end of the market, or at least for the *Daily Worker*, the newspaper of the Communist Party of Great Britain, which purported to speak for the proletarian masses, Alexander could do no wrong. One can imagine the amusement with which the author received a cutting dated 14 December 1961 in which *Rape of the Fair Country* was listed as one of the books recommended in the year about to close. How Alexander chuckled to see that he was rated along with such delights as *Engels–Lafargue Correspondence, Mikhail Tal's Best Games of Chess, Cuba: Hope of a Hemisphere* and *Archaeology in the USSR!*

The several hundred pounds yielded from the initial burst of sales of *Rape of the Fair Country* turned into a thousand, then several thousands, making life at Holywell Crescent comfortable for the three occupants. Alexander did not, however, cease work for another eight years, though he could easily have afforded to do so. Apart from the natural pride of authorship, in the newspaper interviews which followed publication there was little posturing on the question of money. Interviewed by the *Western Mail* five days after publication Alexander declared, 'Money means nothing to me. I already have enough to get by. My life is completely contained with my wife and my small daughter. Money is given to you for helping others, and that is what I shall do with it, since I already have enough to keep me comfortably.'

Mary Morgan of *Reynold's News,* who travelled to the house in Holywell Crescent in February 1959, met a man who, in her own words 'feared fame may change him'. Although deferential in manner Alexander was already demonstrating the deft way he had with interviewers. He told the reporter that he and Rosina rarely entertained and seldom had a night out. 'I spend nearly all my evenings working,' he affirmed. He also revealed what was, for a professional writer, a rather surprising lack of interest in the work of others. 'Before I started writing I wasn't interested in reading. Now I haven't got the time.' Throughout his life he was to maintain that other people's fiction interested him only a little. George Borrow's *Wild Wales* was rarely out of reach and also his favourite work, Edward Fitzgerald's *Rubáiyát of Omar Khayyám,* but right at the end of his life, apart from those works sent to him by Welsh authors hoping for some assistance or favour, his bookshelves were largely filled with his own works. Alexander Cordell would frequently, and with some justification, insist that he was not an intellectual, his organ of choice being the heart rather than the brain. Every good interview should cast a shaft of light on the subject, and Miss Morgan's questions revealed something of which she almost certainly did not realize the importance. As a writer who had identified himself with the Left, and who had been published by Gollancz, Alexander often felt that rather than having served in the British Army in 1936 he should have been with the International Brigades sent to defend the Spanish Republic. This lingering regret surfaced when Alexander answered wistfully in reply to Miss Morgan's question, 'Yes, I'd like to go to Spain. I've had an idea for a novel about the Spanish Civil War which has been worrying me for years.' At the time this statement was made the Spanish Civil War had been resolved in General Franco's favour only twenty years before and was still a live topic among Leftists.

Certainly, Alexander's lifestyle remained modest. The meeting with Miss Morgan was conducted in the Hereford Arms where he drank with his friends once a week. 'Don't get the idea I'm one of those hard-drinking writers,' he told his interviewer. A picture taken of the author and three others show them all smoking pipes but only Alexander clutching a glass of whisky. Life in the officers' mess had left him with a taste for spirits rather than beer, and he was now able to indulge it. Even in the late 1950s drinking spirits was still something of a luxury. The house in Holywell Crescent was comfortable, rather than luxurious, with a piano, record-player and television and, by 1963, a Ford Zephyr car, and, in rapid succesion, a Singer Gazelle, both stylish acquisitions in those days.

To the victor the spoils: Alexander with the Singer Gazelle paid for by *Rape of the Fair Country*'s success.

As they had done in Shrewsbury the Grabers were also acquiring friends. His army days apart, Alexander had never been a big drinker although he looked forward to his weekly visits to the Hereford Arms. The Grabers' new neighbours were congenial. From cheery greetings over the garden fence they soon progressed to visiting the home of Max and Elsie May Donovan at 5 Holywell Crescent. Max was the sort of man to whom the words 'solid' and 'dependable' are generally applied. Of some practical ability, he would help Alexander with household projects and the two families would tour the countryside and picnic in Alexander's car. From the very beginning Alexander was enchanted by Elsie, a little woman of Merthyr stock, with a bright smile and ready laugh. Rosina was as impressed by the Donovans as was Alexander. Neither of the couple had literary pretensions, indeed neither had any discernible literary interests, so Alexander was not threatened or challenged in any way. These were salad days, the best of all possible times. Alexander was deeply in love with Rosina and entranced by Georgina, who was precociously clever with the piano, and he also knew that he was admired and respected by Max and particularly by Elsie.

By 1960 Alexander was already nearing the end of another book which would be *The Hosts of Rebecca*. The reception to *Rape of the*

Fair Country had been so overwhelming that a visit to the United States was being spoken of. In the early sixties Alexander Cordell, as he was generally known by this time, had become adept at living at two levels, his existence compartmentalized. For the reading public he was still the ex-officer, urbane and suave, in his forties, quite old enough to carry off a pipe and often to be seen in cravat and tweed jacket. In this persona, Cordell debated with the Welsh literary establishment and showed occasional streaks of arrogance. In the other he was the friend of the working man and mistrustful of the literary panjandrums. Once, in combative mood he set the literary undergrowth alight and enraged amateur poets and unpublished short-story writers by saying in print that Arts Council subsidies were wasted on 'pub poets'. Indignant letters were sent to the daily papers but, fortunately for Alexander, the matter died a natural death. Otherwise, the reputation of a writer who had put himself so squarely on the side of 'the people' might have been seriously affected. He knew how important it was to keep his public's sympathy and he was never to make a mistake like this again. Henceforth his complaints would be about an ill-defined 'Establishment', which at times seems to have included the Arts Council and the BBC, and it was a convenient scapegoat when he later experienced frustration in getting *Rape of the Fair Country* filmed or televised. In fact, none of Alexander Cordell's work was screened during his lifetime.

This sometimes fractious person would not have been immediately recognizable to the people of mid-Gwent to whom he was an increasingly familiar figure. The £10 motor cycle had long been traded for a car which would take him to the scene of any research pretty much at will. The breathalyzer was still a couple of years in the future. In those days a driver need not be overly concerned about leaving licensed premises after only one pint of beer and in the cheeriness of local pubs Alexander met men who provided many of the facts for his books. He would listen to their stories, but also their speech. Many were not aware that it was not only what they had to say that was being absorbed, but also the manner in which it was said. For such folk Alexander remained 'the man of the people', approachable, modest, quiet and with a face that would light up with encouragement as the tales were told. One month after the publication of *Rape of the Fair Country,* Alexander told the *Abergavenny Chronicle* that he had stopped his motor cycle 'and interviewed every man and woman over the age of seventy and asked them to tell me about the old days'. If it was the cheerfully proletarian Alexander who visited the pubs of Blaenavon, Nantyglo or Brynmawr, it was the middle-class version who was a member of Abergavenny Operatic Society. Music was then, and remains, near the centre of the Welsh psyche. Although English, Alexander was tuned to the same emotional pitch as are many Welsh people, which was, of course, a large part of his success.

What Alexander never mentioned later, and which is remembered by few, is that the author was a member of Abergavenny's Congregational Church. The admission, if admission it was, was made in the same *Abergavenny Chronicle* article. If anything, Alexander's early religious influences had been via the Catholic Marist Brothers who taught him at Tiensin. In his public utterances Alexander was quick to condemn the role of the Church (by which he meant Christianity in general) as being a social instrument used by the ruling and commercial classes to keep the workers quiet. In his *Critique of Hegel* Karl Marx wrote, 'Religion . . . is the opium of the people': Alexander would have sided with those who took that to be a condemnation of religion rather than a neutral observation of fact. And yet he and Rosina had been married at the Congregational Church in Shrewsbury (now the United Reformed Church) a quarter of a century before. The *Abergavenny Chronicle* reference is, as far as can be established, the only reference to organized religion in Alexander's life except the author's own to the Marist Brothers. Towards the end of his life, as the evening wore on and the distance between the neck of a bottle of Famous Grouse and the liquid within got greater, his looks made cherubic by the whisky, Alexander recited more or less word for word the introduction to a book by Frame and Buckingham he had written almost ten years before. 'When my time comes, and having already seen threescore years and ten this cannot be far distant, they can put me down in an orange box, for I was once in love with a girl who wore orange box rope garters . . . for as Taliver Trueblade, my boyhood hero, once declared, "I care not what happens to this carcass once the soul has fled".' Any discussion about spirituality or religion rarely got past that point and Alexander was quick to condemn the Church and to scoff at any suggestion of the afterlife. Strangely, though, he would quite openly talk about seeing ghosts, and references to the supernatural crop up in his works. He was an atheist, but something of a reluctant one. The exuberant story-teller in Alexander would have realized that atheism is dull fare for the imagination. Anyway, he respected the Nonconformist religion of the majority of Welsh people and wanted to identify with it. Doctrine was never a consideration. Definitions are like off-the-peg suits in that they fit only where they touch but if one had to define Alexander's beliefs it would be humanism tinged with mysticism.

He would have scoffed at the idea that some guardian angel was looking after him as the winter of 1959 turned into the spring of the new decade, yet the fingers pecking at the typewriter were charmed. On Christmas Eve 1959 *The Times* listed *Rape of the Fair Country* first in a list of books published that year which had pleased the reviewers. During that year the book had been published in the United States and plans for a visit to that country were consequently speeded up. The book was also translated for publication in eight European countries, but Alexander knew that it was the English-speaking market that really counted. *Rape of the Fair Country* turns on the antipathy between the Welsh working class of the early to middle part of the nineteenth century and its English masters. Substitute the word 'oppressors' for 'masters' and the appeal for some sections of American society becomes clear. Britain may have been America's gallant ally in the recent war but 'England' smacked of cruelty, snobbery, Empire and exploitation. The descendants of those who had fled the British Isles, the Welsh and to a greater extent the Irish, were a ready market for an author who made the shortcomings of the English so obvious. As favourable reviews for *Rape of the Fair Country* continued to dribble in from tiny newspapers in obscure parts of the American West and the money continued to flow into Alexander's bank account, all seemed well with the world.

Yet there was a fear which nagged at the back of the author's mind as he rode the tide of adulation. What if the next book was not as good as the first? Provisionally, he had intended to call *Rape of the Fair Country*'s sequel *Cry of a Fair People* but became convinced that this sounded a trifle weak for a story about people prepared to take militant action against their plight. *The Hosts of Rebecca* was a much better title.

Whether *The Hosts of Rebecca*, when it was published on 20 August 1960, was stylistically as good as or better than *Rape of the Fair Country* is not the job of this book to say. The latter had broken new ground with its south Wales industrial background and its stylistic innovations and this made it a hard act to follow. As the reviews for his second major work came in, Alexander certainly felt as though he had pulled it off. As the favourable reviews for *The Hosts of Rebecca* (*Robe of Honour* in the United States) were collected by the cuttings agency, moves to make its predecessor into a film forged ahead. Welsh-born producer Norman Williams was approached to make the film. Press coverage was gushing. 'Stanley Baker it is!', fanfared Tony Austin in the *Western Mail*. 'Baker, lean, rugged, Welsh and the tough boy of British films is to be Dada, hero of the turbulent, earthy, ironworkers' saga *Rape of the Fair Country* on the screen. And that announcement puts an end to speculation about the possibility of Richard Burton, Trevor Howard, and even Rock Hudson for the role.' *Zulu* was big box-office news that year and Stanley Baker, who took a leading part, was then at the height of his fame, as was Richard Burton. What Austin never knew was that Burton had read the book with a personal, but not professional interest.

That fact emerged eight years after Burton's death when Mike Buckingham and Richard Frame were on holiday in Key West, Florida. In the Hog's Breath bar, on Duval Street, just across from Sloppy Joe's bar, the two were approached by a Californian who overheard their British accents and arranged for them to meet Phillip Burton, whose protégé Richard had been.

When they met, the talk was largely of Richard Burton, although other Welsh literary and dramatic figures threaded in and out of the conversation. It was a couple of hours before Alexander was mentioned, his name coupled as it usually was when being mentioned for the first time with *Rape of the Fair Country*. 'Ah, yes,' Phillip exclaimed. 'Richard was very interested in it and thought it was very good but I remember him shaking his head and saying, "But there's no part in it for me".'

Rape of the Fair Country skimmed like a sloop before a stiff breeze, carrying Alexander's expectations with it. Such critical voices as were raised were scattered to the winds. *Hosts of Rebecca* was received with hardly less heady praise and a film of the first book should have been the most obvious thing in the world. So why did it not happen? A clue is contained in a *Western Mail* report dated 19 February 1962 which states without equivocation that filming at and around Blaenavon was to begin in two months' time. 'While he spent nearly three years on the book,' the unnamed journalist wrote (inaccurately), 'it took Mr Graber just over a fortnight to write the film-script which, he says, makes few changes from the book.' Richard Burton's opinion had no bearing upon the decision not to film the book. That a film-script would not contain a part for him was a private view expressed by a professional actor on a casting matter and did not disparage the book in any way. A filmed version of *Rape of the Fair Country* would seem to be the natural concomitant of the published work, an easy transition from the page to the screen. Yet to this very day no film has been made. The fact of the matter is that having breathed life into the Mortymers, Alexander was reluctant to pass them over to any other creative intelligence for safe keeping. 'Words are like jewels, and you have very few left' was one of his favourite observations which would always be passed on to aspiring authors. He certainly treated the words of *Rape of the Fair Country* – all 100,000 of them – as if they were precious gems, keeping them locked in the cave of his own creativity and refusing to let other lights fall upon them.

All his life Alexander strove for a profound understanding of people and how they acted. He instinctively understood the subliminal desires which drove the characters in his books and which also lit deep and smouldering fires within his readers. More than once he gave Mike Buckingham advice on descriptive writing which included the observation dated 1988, 'Don't say his shirt was bloodied. Say his shirt was starched with blood. It is a liaison with the kitchen.' The odd use of the word 'liaison' apart, the advice is memorable. Kitchens, for Alexander, were a trigger for the deepest associations. Breasts and milk, fire and warmth, darkness and the moon were similarly part of this emotional armoury, but for Alexander their power was released by the spoken word, and he could never see how a film-maker might subtly spin art out of their hidden meanings in his own medium. While it is not true to say that Alexander had an underdeveloped visual sense, his fervid writing life left little time for its expression. He was born in an age long before television and, although he always delighted in the cinema, the films he liked were the commercial box-office hits and not the more thoughtful productions aimed at a more discerning audience. He had never been to see an 'art' film and would not have thought much of one had he been. Alexander's idea of a 'proper' film was epitomized by the epics of his own time, films like *El Cid* or *Cleopatra* with casts of thousands and properties and effects on a Brobdingnagian scale. In Alexander's mind reconstructed furnaces lit up the night sky as hundreds toiled in their infernal-light; thousands of Chartists surged down a Stow Hill in Newport especially reconstructed for the occasion and barely a word was to be dropped from the original book. Each time Alexander saw a proposed film or stage script of an adaptation of his work he was genuinely horrified at the relative slimness of it. It was going to be another Cleopatra with furnaces instead of sphinxes and Welsh workers instead of Nubian slaves or it was going to be nothing at all. In the early post-publication days Alexander could have had the film-makers eating out of his hand had he not been so insistent. It was all or nothing, and he got nothing. Such, though, is the feeling of an author for his work. The filming that was to have begun within weeks in 1962 had not progressed six-and-a-half years later when the

Daily Mirror carried a picture of the singer Mary Hopkin, then eighteen, with Stanley Baker. Baker told the *Mirror* that Miss Hopkin was 'perfect for the part' in his £2,000,000-budget production but did not say which part. The formal offer of a part in *Rape of the Fair Country* was to have reached her 'that morning', according to the newspaper. There is a certain pathos about the accompanying *Mirror* picture, the ageing actor with the rising young star of the pop world. It smacks of having been set up by an agent to keep Baker in the public eye. The offer never came, and whatever part it was that Miss Hopkin was to have been offered has never been played on celluloid to this very day.

The Hosts of Rebecca continues with the Mortymer family in a new setting, the rolling farmland of Carmarthenshire, the main difference being that landowners who erected tolls rather than the ironmasters were the oppressors. As Mam is made to say, 'We ran from Monmouth-shire iron for a bit of peace and we bump into riots all over again.' As early as publication of *The Hosts of Rebecca* Alexander was exhibiting a curious trait which was to remain with him for the rest of his life. On the very eve of publication he told the *South Wales Echo*'s 'Stroller' column, 'I plan to lay down my pen'. By this time Alexander was forty-five. His first book, *A Thought of Honour* had made 'insufficient money to buy a good suit'. *Rape of the Fair Country* had set book-sellers' cash registers tinkling but *The Hosts of Rebecca* was an unknown quantity, which may have caused his nervous and slightly hysterical reaction. In the 'Stroller' piece Alexander tried to laugh off his obvious anxieties by making a weak joke: 'Perhaps laying down my pen is the wrong word. I type all my novels.' But later in the interview he went on to confirm that he intended to stop writing altogether after the publication of 'one, or maybe two' more books, one of which would be set in America. Very many years later it became a standing joke that when Alexander had finished a book he would telephone somebody to say, 'This is the last one, you know'. The reassurances and encouragement which were offered were all part of the game. Alexander came to have some ambivalence about *Rape of the Fair Country* which had made his name, yet had set a standard very early on in his writing career which he feared might be hard to match. At various times he would dismiss *Rape of the Fair Country* as something he had just tossed off and claim that another book such as *To Slay the Dreamer* was his favourite. Such assertions never had the ring of sincerity about them. He need not have worried about the *Rape of the Fair Country*'s successor. *The Hosts of Rebecca* achieved respectable sales and was reprinted several times, including a Victor Gollancz hardback reprint in 1983.

With his second novel under his belt the author had no real intention of giving up the craft which was reaping not inconsiderable rewards and had come to dominate his life. Books and writing were indispensable. The humdrum job as a War Office quantity surveyor was beginning to irk. Even so, fame had not made Alexander reckless. He knew that two more things were to be wrung from his nine-to-five existence. The first was that if he stayed in his post until the age of fifty, which he would attain in 1964, he would get a pension. Secondly, Britain still had considerable overseas interests in those days, one of which was Hong Kong. In the Crown colony living was cheap and easy and it might be possible to cross into Communist China, a land he had loved since boyhood. The government machine which had employed Alexander ever since he first joined the Army in 1932 had one more part to play before its usefulness to the fully fledged author was done. More immediately, though, Alexander Cordell, who had taken his name from an American, had to visit the largest English-speaking country in the world, the biggest market for his works and the ultimate source of most of the world's film money.

Chapter Nine

On 6 February 1961, Alexander took off from London Heathrow bound ultimately for Pittsburgh upon the invitation of that city's Welsh Club. He planned to research a new book there. Even as late as the 1960s there was still a feeling that America was a land to be discovered, rather than merely visited. Although in almost every way more technically advanced than post-war Britain it still, for most English-speaking people, represented a kind of frontier. Llanellen and Abergavenny and Garndyrus seemed cosy little places as day broke and the airliner's contrail unzipped the cold blue sky of the Canadian Arctic, the tiny point of silver at its tip forging ever southwards across the seemingly endless empty miles. The leaving of the British Isles had not been an entirely routine matter. Alexander had stopped off in Ireland, visiting Connemara to research some of the background for what was to become *Race of the Tiger*, his work in progress. While he was in Ireland an aeroplane crashed near Shannon airport. Alexander heard of the crash on the local news but then seems to have filed it in the back of his mind as one of the many things to tell Rosina about his trip when they next spoke. For reasons of economy, and the relative difficulty of making transatlantic calls in those days, Alexander and Rosina had agreed to be sparing in their use. The unfortunate thing was that while the crash was of only passing interest to Alexander, something to mention casually when he eventually did call, to Rosina it had become an agony of waiting to be reassured that her husband's name was not on the list of casualties. Had Alexander been fully aware of what anxieties had been put in train by the lack of news reaching Rosina and the effect upon her health, he would certainly have cut short the eighteen-day visit.

Ireland, where he had spent some days touring was not so very different from the Abergavenny he had recently left. America was a different prospect altogether, vast, foreign and daunting. There was a palpable excitement in the Aer Lingus plane, a quickening of the pulses as it began to descend towards the New York skyline. 'So this is New York! A colossus, a sprawling edifice, a riotous roar of a city of steepled skyscrapers and monumental blocks gilded in its winter of 13 degrees, its sidewalks piled with snow,' Alexander wrote shortly after landing at Idlewild, now Kennedy Airport, and pitching into the rush of a city that made even London seem provincial. Even in the first whirligig moments Alexander still kept his ear for language, listening to the American cadences around him. In those days transatlantic travel was for the relatively few and it was not long before he had passed through baggage reclaim and immigration and was outside in the biting cold looking for a taxi that would take him to the Berkshire Hotel in downtown New York.

The change of mood and tempo was like a rich sauce to his imagination, for within a couple of weeks he was writing of these moments:

> Raked from the blood-red cloud layers of the transatlantic flight, after six hours of an unrelenting chase of the setting sun one is plunged into this bedlam of a city . . . sleek limousines and slick taxis are weaving in a breakneck lust for living; horns are blasting and headlights flashing; the crowds barging outside the Golden Door restaurant, pale-faced as ghosts, chattering in foreign tongues in the melting-pot of a city which daily disgorges and absorbs its countless creeds and nationalities from the corners of the world. You are injected into an inferno of commotion, a roaring rat-race of unbelievable speed and fury that snatches at you and carries you along on its tide, willing or not.

And Alexander was willing, hungry for the experience, his pen quickened by the speed and bustle but also by something which lies deeper than that, which might be reflected in the cold light glinting from the refracting lens of the skyscraper tops, a light which suggests enormous distances and strikes the soul in a minor key. Despite being assailed by these new sounds and images the author in Alexander was working at full bore. Authors, he said, must listen a lot and say little. Just as several years before he had listened to the Welsh wives at Abergavenny market, he was now listening to the high staccato chatter of the Spanish-speaking Puerto Rican airport-workers and the New York accent with its slight intonation of Yiddish and its remote ancestor, the Cockney of London. Alexander was very soon to be reminded that it was not he who was discovering a new world, rather a new world that was engulfing him, a representative of just one of the nationalities in that teeming city. A cab slewed to a halt and Alexander bundled his suitcase in and followed it, asking the cabbie for the Berkshire Hotel. 'The *Bark*shire?', the cabbie shot back. The man consulted his map and grinned at the newcomer in the back seat. 'You said "Barkshire" Mister. You got the sound wrong. Fifty-Second Street.'

Relieved that there were at least some passing similarities in the languages, Alexander reclined in the Yellow Cab as it took him to the nerve-centre of the city that never sleeps, a maelstrom of lights and noise. So hectic were the events that Alexander, in a flustered moment, even found himself forced into a defence of Winston Churchill, a politician whom he did not admire. In between lowering his window to shout oaths at pedestrians and from the corner of his mouth that was not occupied by a cigar, the driver asked Alexander if he 'went' for Churchill adding, 'Great guy. We get him on the TV over here.' Alexander admitted it was with a certain smugness that he replied that Winston Churchill had been great even before television had been invented, but, to avoid any accusation of Limey smartness, had gone on to ask the driver whether he was familiar with the war-leader's speeches.

'I was treated to a dissertation by this young man with the cigar', he later recalled. 'He was only working as a cabbie part-time to raise the money to get him through college. This pleased me for some reason even though I only got small change out of ten dollars, which was about £3.75 in those days.'

At the Berkshire Alex was signed in, told that his room would cost him $14 a night (very nearly a week's pay for the average working Welshman) and placed in a bedroom at the rear of the hotel where, immediately, he was attacked by the exhaustion and melancholy well known to travellers. 'In the solitary confines of a foreign bedroom, the loneliest place in the world, I sat and longed for the sight and sound of my distant Abergavenny, the cool beauty of the Usk . . . where the Blorenge changes colour with each new rush of the sun,' he wrote in a *South Wales Argus* article after his return.

Despite this temporary gloom his impressions of this new country were overwhelmingly favourable, to the point that he seems at one point to have donned rose-tinted spectacles. Emerging from his hotel next day, having spent the evening counting his dollars and 'wondering what they did with vagrants in this country', he met a black beggar.

I gave him half-a-dollar, but Joe Marrinan, the red-coated bartender I talked to said I was wrong, for there was no need for anyone to starve in New York. I didn't believe Joe at the time but I do now, for there is an excellent social service and numerous charities to which white or coloured people can appeal, though of course the whole nation appears envious of our National Health Service, and rightly.

With the wisdom that hindsight brings we can forgive the naïveté. Forty years ago even the most prosperous parts of Britain seemed drab and unexciting compared with much of the United States and certainly New York. The noise from the jazz bars, the ceaseless roar and honking of the traffic and the Babel tower of voices were like a delicious assault on the senses, overload for the critical faculties. Even so, Alexander with his keen eye for injustice was not seduced entirely. 'I found a true spirit of democracy. It is not uncommon to see a rich man talking on a corner with a poor man – in one case a coloured roadsweeper. But the only real barrier to social acceptance is the Almighty Dollar.'

In Pittsburgh Alexander was hosted and toasted, singing for his supper as is the time-honoured way with British and European intellectuals and writers visiting the United States. After he had recovered from his initial culture shock, Alexander launched upon the American scene with gusto. Ever since the war he had had a high regard for the American 'can do' approach to life which in many ways mirrored his own. Many years later he would recall his days at the Orford Battle Area in Suffolk when he was a Sapper officer and some Americans were sent to the British Army on detachment. 'I was giving a lecture about bridge building when one of the young American officers politely interjected and said, "That can't be right, Sir" and got his slide rule working and within a flash proved that what I had been saying couldn't work in reality.' There was a typical Alexander ending to this story. 'I let him make his point before mentioning that the bridge may not have been workable according to the slide rule, but we had actually proved it in battle.' It was typical of Alexander's generosity to let the young have their say and to deliver only the mildest reproof. In very much the same spirit he gave America the benefit of whatever doubts he may have harboured.

The book Alexander was in the United States to research was provisionally entitled *The Pittsburgh Story* before he hit on the more imaginative *Race of the Tiger*. Much of his work was done in libraries and museums, although he did meet the former leader of the American mineworkers' union, John L. Lewis, who was of Welsh extraction. If New York was flash and tinsel, Pittsburgh was solid money, made from steel. Alexander always had a good eye for territory, imagining how this greatest among the world's steel towns grew up in the fork between the Ohio and the Monongahela rivers, four hundred miles from Philadelphia. The pace of the city he found slower than New York, and the people even more to his liking. 'Irish, Scotch, Welsh and Slav is mixed with Indian blood to give a race more like the British that any I have ever encountered,' Alex said approvingly. A little later in his career, when writing *The Sinews of Love*, Alexander tried to make a connection between the Welsh and the Chinese. Ethnology, the study of human races, was not his strongest suit. In common with other literary travellers to the United States, he found the hospitality almost embarrassing, lavished upon him particularly by those of Welsh descent. The Welsh had made their way in this city perhaps more than anywhere else on the face of the earth, he noted, infiltrating the innermost core of the city's cultural, political and business life. Among the first to greet him was Mrs Collette Thomas, leader of the Welsh Club, who in fact maintained contact with friends in Abercarn in Gwent and who presided at a dinner at which Alexander was the guest speaker.

'The talk at that dinner was of Wales, the mother country; of Merthyr and Dowlais, Carmarthen and Cardigan; they sang Welsh hymns and songs, they spoke Welsh poetry.' A couple of days later the Deputy Lieutenant-Governor of Pennsylvania, Mr J. Morgan Davies, who wore his Welsh ancestry proudly, was guest of honour at the Welsh Club's annual dinner held at the city's Hilton Hotel three days after St David's Day. Although Alexander would have been too polite to say so, it was a cause of some frustration that the necessity to meet Pittsburgh's élite was eating into his study time. He was speaking to captains of industry when what he really wanted to do, for the purposes of *Race of the Tiger*, was to get amongst the poor bloody infantry. Some of the frustration may have surfaced during an interview with an unnamed tycoon, 'who asked me nostalgically whether the sheep still wandered in the streets of Dowlais and did the mountain ponies compete with the women of Ebbw Vale in window-gazing on Saturday winter nights'.

'Come home and see', I said to him. 'You have the money.' He told me that he had been in Wales the year before but it didn't make his sense of longing any easier. 'The remedy for that sickness is in your own hands', I told him. The longing for Wales of these displaced people had a greater impact on me, I think, than anything else I found in Pennsylvania. I tried to explain this emotion in a broadcast I made from New York but I do not think I succeeded.

Nor did America succeed in completely entrancing the author who, upon his return to Abergavenny and his writing desk with a view of the Blorenge mountain, jotted down an observation that the fury of the New World, despite its sincerity and hospitality, was a very poor substitute for the calmness of the Old World and 'the balm of its tranquillity'. There was little tranquillity, though, for the author who flew home to a desperately ill wife. The air crash at Shannon which he had passed on as a snippet of news had been received by Rosina with great anxiety. The medical details are vague and Alexander may well have understated their severity but the story given to the *South Wales Argus* was that Rosina had developed an ulcer following news of the plane crash. That seems unlikely. She must have had the ulcer for some time for it to have reached a stage of bursting. She was taken swiftly to hospital and given blood transfusions and had regained consciousness by the time Alexander touched down in the United Kingdom. Still, it was a nasty scare and the beginning of a run of bad health which was ultimately to lead to Rosina's premature death.

On 14 February – St Valentine's Day – one edition of the *Argus* contained a news story about Alexander's return to the United Kingdom under the headline 'Good News and Bad for Gwent Author'. The bad news was, of course, Rosina's illness. The good news was that the contract had been signed for the film rights of *Rape of the Fair Country*. Less than two years after publication of the book a film still seemed a reasonable prospect, although Alexander must have secretly been worrying about whether a film would in fact materialize. 'Gwent Author's Book to be Filmed', or a variation thereof, was a frequent headline over the coming years.

On the same day as the news article, the *Argus* ran a feature story on the inside pages in which Rosina, much recovered, gave an interview to Josephine Type. The journalist was a Merthyr girl, tough and resilient but with a fluent writing style that Alexander came to admire. In 1961, Josephine, who was to remain at the *Argus* for another quarter of a century and to become features editor before succumbing to cancer, was approaching maturity as a reporter. In the terrible Six Bells colliery disaster she had interviewed survivors, families and rescuers, keeping her emotions on a tight rein and writing in a terse style which in its very spareness emphasized the scale of the tragedy even as the bodies were carried past. A decade before the first stirrings of women's liberation, Rosina's interview gave a picture of the perfectly compliant housewife. No mention of any illness was made in the article, although the accompanying picture in which she is reading a letter with the young Georgina looking over her shoulder shows her wearing a strained expression.

In 1961 the couple had been married twenty-four years, ten of which had been spent at Llanellen or Holywell Crescent. Rosina told the reporter, 'We love this part of the country and don't ever want to leave.' With *Rape of the Fair Country* a runaway success, *The Hosts of Rebecca* performing satisfactorily and an American book which was to be *Race of the Tiger* in the planning stage, Alexander could have made the break with government service and settled down to a life of writing. In not doing so he was following the advice he would give to aspiring writers for the rest of his life. A man of forty-seven has another eighteen years to go before he qualifies for the state pension. This was a long haul which Alexander never intended making. His quantity surveying job was undemanding and in three years he would be fifty and entitled to retire with a pension. A cautious man in many respects, Alexander saw the sense in hanging on for another three years to claim the government pension which would provide an adequate safety-net in the event of his literary income slowing to a trickle. It is surprising that Josephine Type never asked about Alexander's financial arrangements. In a little town like Abergavenny the people who saw him with a brand-new car and other signs of greatly increased prosperity and were aware of his growing reputation must surely have wanted to know when he was going to make the financial jump. Rosina spoke to Josephine Type about Alexander's work methods. Her husband was neither temperamental nor a recluse, she said. 'He just goes and sits in the dining room and types away. We try not to disturb him but if either Georgina or I want to talk to him he never minds us going into the room. As a matter of fact, he cannot write unless he has his family about him in the house.'

While Alexander was writing, she got on with the 'little jobs' around the house, and a 'spot of gardening'. Sometimes her advice was sought. 'Alex will often read chapters to me as he completes them. At one time I never said anything, just listened, but now if I don't like what he writes I really slate him and he values my opinion. At other times when he is working on a plot he always listens to any ideas I might come forward with.' About one thing she was adamant: 'He will not alter facts. Some of the things he wrote about in *Rape of the Fair Country* were terribly hard and brutal. I told him so but he wouldn't change that aspect because he said it was a true picture of the times.'

Rosina revealed that they did not go out a great deal socially (presumably Alexander's visits to the Hereford, his local, fell into a different category) but she maintained an interest in a club for the blind, another for the disabled, as well as being a mainstay of the welfare section of the Red Cross. Later in life Alexander, who used to work in the morning and leave the rest of the day free for driving out into the country, or going for a meal or picnicking, did not like to be disturbed while he was working. About Rosina's contribution to his work there is no doubt. She, and later Elsie Donovan, were precisely the class of readers he wrote for.

The good news part of the 'good news, bad news' equation which greeted Alexander upon his return from the United States evaporated that summer. Norman Williams, the British producer who had signed for the film rights, declared in July 1961 that he had failed to find a British backer and would therefore be looking across the Atlantic, perhaps with a co-operative or cost-sharing venture in view. John Ford, who had directed *How Green Was My Valley* (the book by Richard Llewellyn with whom sometimes Alexander was compared) had been approached and had agreed to read the script but that, too, came to nothing. Alexander's almost brooding possessiveness of his work and his inability to edit and rewrite for the screen had led to another chance slipping by.

All this time Alexander's profile at home was being raised. Barely a month went by without his being mentioned in the *Abergavenny Chronicle* and interviews with the *South Wales Argus*, the evening newspaper which covers Gwent, and the *Western Mail*, the national newspaper of Wales, were frequent. More times than he might have wished he was asked to give talks to societies and clubs. It is generally a thankless task. Alexander was a natural speaker who, once warmed to his theme, let the natural force of words and his character take over. This was preceded, though, by considerable anxiety. Sometimes he would type out a whole speech and be annoyed that this was effort that could have been better employed in writing fiction. Nevertheless, he did it with good grace and for the not altogether altruistic reason that the people who were going to listen to his speeches and lectures were the ones that would end up reading his books. Sometimes he was to be persuaded into activities which were not quite in keeping with his image. A feminist before his time, Alexander had no liking of beauty contests, something we do not see much of today but which were popular as late as the 1970s. In October 1961 he was persuaded to share the judges' table, together with Anne Lambton, a well-known fashion designer of the period, and Ossie Wheatley, then captain of Glamorgan County Cricket Club, for the selection of Miss Bri-Nylon 1962. Prudently perhaps, Alexander did not make any comment for inclusion in *Signpost*, the official works magazine of British Nylon Spinners which was based at Mamhilad, near Pontypool, thus giving the impression that he was less than enthused by the event. He was pictured on the front page, though, kissing the cheek of seventeen-year-old Pat Woodhouse, from Doncaster, who took first prize. The corniness of the evening was accentuated by the trumpeters supplied by the Royal Air Force training base at nearby St Athan.

The Hosts of Rebecca and *Race of the Tiger* had dispelled completely doubts which Alexander sometimes harboured, that he was a 'one-book wonder'. *Rape of the Fair Country* had broken a mould, which is considerably more than most authors ever achieve. The books which came after were technically the equal of *Rape* and the sales sent the author's stock soaring not only in the United Kingdom but, with *Race of the Tiger*, in the United States. But it was neither of the most populous

English-speaking countries in the world that attracted him in the mid-1960s. Alexander Cordell was to be fifty years old in September 1964 and eligible for a civil-service pension. As the first sense of his own mortality gathered about him, it was China that called, that vast land in which many of his childhood memories were fixed. At home, the mid-sixties were a period in which time seemed to play weird tricks. Beatlemania was sweeping Britain, America and Europe. Bob Dylan had released the first of his fervently anti-war songs in *North Country Blues* and it was the time of Motown music, originating in the motor town of Detroit, of which the Supremes were then the leading exponents. The youth culture which would come to dominate the rest of the twentieth century was launched in a clash of electric guitars and a haze of psychedelic drugs. To Alexander it must have seemed like another world. The war had been over less than twenty years.

Although *Rape of the Fair Country* was undoubtedly required reading for many on the political Left, then in its ascendancy, the author and his family lived a life not entirely isolated but distanced from the radical-student culture which was a part of the 1960s. On 4 April 1964 Georgina Graber was the piano soloist at St George's School where, musically, she was the most promising pupil. The cool notes, played with precision, of her Bach (*Largo* and *Allegro*) and Chopin's *Prelude* seemed to Alexander like a sigh from a civilization that was breaking up into a clashing discord. Britain was being engulfed by a permissiveness which sat ill with the old soldier side of Alexander. In China, though, the Red Guards of Chairman Mao were tearing at the roots of their ancient culture in the cause of the advancement of the proletariat, and that was much more to his taste, particularly if it could be observed from the comfort and security of Hong Kong, at the expense of Her Majesty's Government, and might provide the material for yet another book.

The MV *Glenearn* which left Southampton bound for the Far East that May with Alexander, Rosina and Georgina aboard was a little capsule of fast disappearing values afloat on a sea of change. Principally a cargo vessel designed to carry a few dozen passengers, she was a ship of middling size with one funnel and large holds at the stern and of a kind that had been plying that route for three-quarters of a century. Her human cargo comprised people of the middling sort; not rich merchants who could afford to fly or senior officials of government or the military, but the civil servants and newspaper editors, doctors, shop managers and school teachers who were the sergeants and lieutenants of colonial administration. In those days a civil servant travelling to Hong Kong might reasonably expect a large and generally efficient administration to sort out such things as accommodation and storage of one's effects while on a foreign tour. The Graber family had been given the required injections and Alexander had been issued with a green card advising him that since his blood group was 'O' and therefore usefully versatile he should carry the card at all times. All worries had been removed by a government which took paternal care of its employees. In Abergavenny, close to the material which had provided him with inspiration for *Rape of the Fair Country*, it had been possible almost to forget the civil service, the demands of which occupied his working day. In the official world of forms and reports, procedures and hierarchies of which the *Glenearn* was a part he was thrown back into a world from which his need for escape was urgent. By this time Alexander had been a public servant of one kind or another for more than thirty years, and was heartily sick of it. While some aspects of modern culture at home, such as pop music, had left him cold, other things such as the growing radicalism had impinged upon him. In particular, his deep respect for women engendered a hatred of concubinage, which he saw as being no better than sexual slavery.

On landing at Hong Kong Alexander and family were met by civil service personnel officers and taken to their new quarters at Royden Court on Repulse Bay. The cargo in the mean time was swung outboard by the dock cranes and carted up to Graber's rented establishment. The real cargo, though, the series of as yet unconnected thoughts and ideas, still many months from any coherent form, was inside Alexander's head. In a year or so it would emerge as *The Sinews of Love*, a book which, with much justification, Alexander considered to be the equal of *Rape of the Fair Country* and one which, in terms of sympathy and affection, treated China in the way the earlier novel had treated Wales. As a child Alexander had stored away many images of China, both of landscape and feeling, which was to inform his writing and bring to it the true depth of feeling apparent in his prose. With *The Sinews of Love* it was time to give something back. After some months the author's proof copy arrived and a month after that was on its way back to England with a hundred or so careful amendments. A few weeks after that the cover design was done and the presses were ready to roll. The first part of Alexander's literary life had come to a triumphant conclusion and a new phase was beginning.

Chapter Ten

Pei Sha, the little Chinese fisher-girl, was, of all Alexander's characters, the one he loved best. Never before had the writer spent so much time endowing his female characters with actions and feeling. *The Sinews of Love* is remarkable in that the few male characters are either insensitive or lecherous, grasping or weak. The similarities with *Rape of the Fair Country* are too obvious to miss and start with the very first line: 'Hong Kong held its breath at the end of the Great Heat. For in the month of September, in the year I was fifteen, there came a big wind from the sea, a sea-bitch . . .' *Rape of the Fair Country* opens with the words 'That June stands clear in my mind' and continues, 'For apart from it being the month Mrs Pantrych went into the heather with Iolo Milk . . .' In each, the month helps to set the scene. The summer in *Rape of the Fair Country* is drowsy and heavy with expectancy as if thunder is threatened. In *The Sinews of Love* it is the typhoon that is imminent, the 'sea-bitch' that will make orphans of Pei Sha, Orla, their brothers Hui and the baby Tuk Un and Suelen, the family's adopted sister. Papa, who is carried away by the storm together with the proceeds of the sale of Orla, and Chu Po San, the junkmaster to whom the orphaned family are apprenticed, between them share many of the characteristics of Dada in *Rape of the Fair Country* in that they deal with the world as it is, not as they would like it to be. A reader coming from the Welsh book to the Chinese will almost certainly draw similarities between the fiery Morfydd and Suelen.

From the family flat, H8, Royden Court, above Repulse Bay, Alexander would wander at will through a Hong Kong that was already a tinselly commercial capital, but still a place where ancient rhythms dictated the daily lives of millions of the ordinary working folk for whom he had such a high regard. So closely did he identify the historical lot of the Welsh and the Chinese that he several times attempted to construct a racial theory which encompassed them both. Alexander's pronouncements on matters of ethnography owed much to imagination and very little, if anything at all, to fact. One of his wilder adventures in this direction took a book entitled *The Historical Basis of Welsh Nationalism* as a starting-point. Swallowing wholesale the theory that 'Cymro' for Welshman was from Gomero, which was in turn from Gomer, the son of Japheth, the son of Noah, he immediately concluded that the history of the Welsh could be traced back to the Flood. 'There will be no true resurrection of Wales', he would maintain, 'until she has the truth of her origins.' Any attempt to explain the prehistoric occupation of Britain by a people of Central European stock was doomed to failure, for Alexander had a much more exotic origin in mind. 'Experts' (who were never named) supported his view that the Celts were 'basically Oriental, to my mind irrefutably Chinese, and probably one of the oldest people on earth.' In the matter of novel-writing Alexander had need to defer to only a handful. In the matter of racial theory he would have any self-respecting scientist reaching for his handkerchief, either to hide his laughs or wipe away the tears. The Chinese and the Welsh loved poetry, but in terms of humour were too sensitive to laugh at themselves. Both liked singing, and some Chinese enjoyed a simple form of rugby. Add to that a pinch of Chinese mythology and you surely have one of the most bizarre theories for the origins of the Welsh ever put forward. Differences between the Chinese and the Welsh, he said, were so small as to be scarcely worth expressing. 'The Chinese housewife, for instance, sews from left to right with the right hand, considering it dangerous to let the needle fly into space less she inadvertently prick the dragon on a festival day.' In some parts of China, Alexander maintained, a form of rugby was played with an inflated pig's bladder. Added to this the Welsh had (the actual figures were never produced) a higher birthrate than the rest of Europe and the argument was deemed to be conclusive.

A half-competent demographer would no doubt dismantle the last assertion in a matter of moments but if the argument had little regard for the truth it had an important place in the scheme of things as far as the author's imagination was concerned. Womanhood was at the centre of creation and in China, as in Wales, women were at the suffering centre of society. 'China, like Wales, is a matriarchal state. The men think they run the place but in fact it's the women who are the strength every time,' he asserted in the late eighties when dining with Frame and Buckingham at the Sleepy Panda, his favourite Chinese restaurant in Wrexham. 'The Chinese woman has a baby on her back, one by her hand and another in her belly. It's the women who have to be reckoned with.' A metaphorical keyhole which allowed a peep into Alexander's subconscious would reveal a place where the womb was the wellspring of all creation and creativity. Alexander's success was precisely because he could get near to the cycle of birth, feeding and death.

Alexander's enthusiasm for all things Chinese sometimes led into amusing by-ways. Occasionally, after the second bottle of wine was dispatched, he would attempt to converse with the waiters and waitresses in his own, highly idiosyncratic version of Cantonese of which the only discernible word was 'Missy' when spoken to a young woman. These linguistic adventures were received with good-natured amusement although the bewilderment of new members of staff who had never been exposed to it before was obvious. Alexander was no kind of linguist at all. A smattering of French and a small amount of Cantonese, the quality of which seemed suspect, seems to have been his total linguistic achievement. However imperfect, the Cantonese would have been seen as a courtesy by the Chinese people he visited at work and in their homes. Rosina, as she had done in Britain, joined various charities and to some extent enjoyed the life of an officer's lady but Alexander would rarely be seen in European clubs, gin-and-tonic in hand. In *The Sinews of Love* the mind's eye can see the scales which encrust the fish-wives' arms like sequins and smell the fish-sheds in the heat and see the eyes of the landed catches change, in death, to a milky blankness. As a writer Alexander Cordell knew it was his business to be in such places, to smell the smells and pick up the pitch of the conversation. He was only doing, in a much more exotic location, what he had been doing at Abergavenny market ten years before.

So deeply was China impressed upon Alexander's consciousness that it was only discovered after his death that a second book was to have been set there. The fact is revealed in the carbon copy of a letter retrieved from among Alexander's papers after his death and dated 1954. The novel was to have been called *China Mission*. The manuscript was submitted to Gollancz within a year of the completion of his first book and returned with a fulsome and encouraging rejection note, but a rejection none the less. Typically, Alexander turned the rejection into a lesson and concluded that his theme and background had too heavily overlain the narrative. Among Alexander's personal mottoes was 'Stitch, stitch, stitch', by which he meant two things. First, nothing should be wasted within the structure of the book and all loose ends should be neatly tied away. Secondly, no words one has set down and troubled to write should ultimately be without a market. Alexander turned the rejection into an article for *Writer* magazine. 'Lack of artistic detachment and a hammering of my theme, about which I feel so strongly, cost me *China Mission*, a novel upon which I was congratulated in every other respect', he wrote in the covering letter to the editor. The actual article deals with the Sirens that had lured many novelists onto the rocks, the over-confidence that follows first publication. 'I was at fever pitch', he wrote of the weeks following *A Thought of Honour*.

I had things to say which they'd read and like it – or else. (Oh, beware of these heated creations, these inspired avenues down which the soul gallops – into a cul-de-sac). And beware too, of a theme which, perhaps subconsciously, your mind has been labouring over perhaps for years without expression . . . But let's be fair. I planned the book well and wrote it well. Its background was China. The story began at the time of Japan's invasion, the 'double seventh' of 7/7/37. This war, like any other, resulted in thousands of children being rendered orphans and homeless. Their urgent need was the <u>motivation</u> of the novel. Then I invented a down-and-out British engineer, James Bamford who has lost his religion and self-respect in the fumes of whisky. The 'plot sentence' is that a degenerate man accepts his moral obligation when the needs of children are presented to him in a manner which forbids escape and thus finds his soul and his God.

The book failed because Alexander allowed it to become a political tract.

I dragged in the superlatives to describe my own emotions. I, not Bamford, heard the ricochets when the children's barge was machine-gunned. I became hostile to everyone who did not assist my labours for the children of China and made their omissions a political issue . . . Personal sacrifice for helpless children was the order of the day. When Pei, my Chinese girl, aged five, was at the point of death . . . (note my own girl is the same age . . .) I described the scene with such emotion that I almost wept. Strange that Bamford, who was also at the bedside, appeared comparatively unaffected.

Evidently Pei Sha already had an existence prior to her appearance in *The Sinews of Love* and it is interesting to note that his affection for the character is in part a reflection of the love for his own daughter, Georgina. It is the wry last sentence which gives the best insight into the mind of the writer. Bamford is a mere spectator in a book which is supposed to be about him. Alexander had learned what he would henceforth consider an axiom of literature which is that the characters must seem to act independently of the author. 'For me, in future, the detached eye. If I boil within, nobody will learn it save through the characters. Months of labour wasted but a good lesson learned,' he ruefully noted. Alexander had learned, the hard way. Never again would he allow his characters to become mouthpieces for his own thoughts and opinions.

If there was a cloud on Alexander's horizon in the mid-1960s it was Rosina's health. A burst ulcer at the time of his American visit had given her further trouble in Hong Kong and for much of their eighteen-month stay she had been in some discomfort. Alexander was at first angered, but very quickly thereafter fascinated, by an incident on a boat in Hong Kong harbour when he mentioned to the Chinese skipper that his wife had been quite seriously ill. Instead of offering the normal platitudes, the skipper started laughing. 'Why are you laughing?', he asked, and the skipper replied: 'I am laughing to cheer you up.' The incident underscored the difference between the Western and Chinese approaches to sickness and death. It was a story he often retold when speaking of Chinese stoicism.

In the spring of 1966 the family sailed for home. Alexander had served long enough to collect a civil service pension and his inclinations were to set up as a self-employed writer. As the boat left Hong Kong harbour for the long trip back to the United Kingdom, doubts about his future began to insinuate themselves. To continue in the civil service would at least mean security. In those days the civil service was a job for life, a virtual sinecure for those able to thrive within its labyrinthine and occasionally bizarre culture. *Rape of the Fair Country* had made sufficient money for Alexander to hint at a personal fortune counted in tens of thousands but there was absolutely no guarantee that sort of money would ever come his way again. And yet, Alexander's zeal for fiction was incandescent and by 1966 had driven out most other considerations, his family apart. At the age of fifty-two with one best-seller and two other books which had achieved respectable sales, he must have thought it was now or never. In fact the die had been cast. He had told the ministry (by this time the three service ministries had been merged into the Ministry of Defence) that he wished to resign and during his latter days in Hong Kong had arranged for the purchase of number 7 Westaway Drive, Hakin, a district of Milford Haven in west Wales. Alexander must have smiled at the thought of moving into another house with the number 7. The house in Holywell Crescent which bore that number had seen happiness and burgeoning success so another number 7 was seen as a good omen.

Ever since the publication of *A Thought of Honour* many years before, Alexander had been something of a local celebrity, called upon to talk to ladies' institutes, writers' circles and to give Workers' Educational Association lectures. Since he had made his living from the people of Gwent, Alexander knew that he could not refuse requests to talk to those who were effectively his subject. Alexander knew that once back in Gwent a resumed round of talks and lectures would put unacceptable strains upon him. With Rosina's ill health increasing there seemed only one sensible course of action. Quite early in his writing career Alexander had realized it can be very difficult for an author to live on his own 'patch'. On the other hand to move away from it was to court accusations of desertion. Hong Kong had removed him from Abergavenny and had given him the time to work out his tactics. His plan would be to move back to Wales but to somewhere sufficiently remote from Gwent so as to be able to accept invitations on his own terms. Milford Haven, then three hours away by road, provided the ideal location. Ever since his recuperation at Harlech and his occasional wartime and post-war visits to Borth, Alexander had been in love with west Wales. Milford Haven put a certain distance between him and the more persistent of his admirers and with its nearby magnificent coastal scenery provided both inspiration and some beautiful locations for family picnics. Besides, there was another Chinese book brewing away and he did not yet want to be distracted with thoughts of Gwent. It was very much a case of absence making the heart grow fonder.

The Bright Cantonese was published in 1967, at the height of the Cold War, the year in which the Secretary General of the United Nations, U Thant, predicted war between the United States and China. In south-east Asia the war had in fact turned decidedly hot with the largest American deployment since the Second World War pitched against the North Vietnamese. Alexander's visit to the Chinese mainland in the last months of 1966, while he was still in Hong Kong, had been his first in forty-five years. Even though he was still in government service and aware of the fact that visits to Communist China were frowned upon, the opinion of his bosses would not have worried him greatly. He had, after all, sufficient money to buy his independence. Impressions of his visit were published in the *Listener* and a radio talk broadcast by the BBC Home Service. China was described approvingly. Politically, Alexander had turned very much against the West and generally felt that those who attacked China for being totalitarian did so through ignorance, or through fear that what he considered to be a morally superior philosophy might one day destroy their privileges. It is always easy to look back from our comfortable viewpoint in the years following the events in Tienanmen Square and accuse authors who accepted Peking's hospitality of naïvety. This is to ignore the fact that, in Britain, tens of thousands of students describing themselves as Maoists were waving Mao's *Little Red Book* and dreaming of revolution. Untypically in terms of post-war British foreign policy

Britain had declined to assist America with its fight in the Far East and many people, not least Alexander, viewed the American position with alarm and concern.

The Bright Cantonese (*The Deadly Eurasian* in the United States) was the nearest Alexander ever got to writing a thriller as the term is generally understood. There are heroines and atom bombs and – as was *de rigeur* – the shadow of the CIA is everywhere. The book has a pacy plot, terse fast-moving dialogue and falls outside the mainstream of Alexander's work; for this reason it tends to get overlooked. For the remainder of his life Alexander continued to take an interest in China but the literary seam which went back to the magazine short stories was thinning. Two more books, *Dream and the Destiny*, published in 1975 and set against the background of Mao's Long March, and *The Dreams of Fair Women* (1993) were to be written before it was exhausted.

Liberated from paid employment, Alexander was, upon his return from Hong Kong and his establishment at Milford Haven, finally free of his velvet handcuffs. Since the early 1930s he had been either a soldier or a civil servant. Government service had taken a substantial chunk out of his upper thigh, but it had generously rewarded him with a good salary, the rank of Major, and far more than either of those things, the time to write. It was with some trepidation that the writer left the comfort and security of government service behind him and set out on a perilous new career.

Chapter Eleven

The period in Milford Haven was a period of quiet consolidation. Increasingly, as the royalties from *Rape of the Fair Country*, *The Hosts of Rebecca*, *Race of the Tiger*, *The Sinews of Love* and *The Bright Cantonese* flowed steadily in, Alexander found himself in need of services provided by the financial institutions he so much despised. In financial matters Alexander proceeded cautiously, buying luxuries only when he was sure he could afford it. By the late 1960s he had reached a high plateau in his life, a time when the early slopes had been achieved, and he could look far across a fertile plain, with only the most distant glimpse of further heights in the far distance. With increasing fame he was aware that some people might through jealousy, or greed, or the sort of perverseness that sometimes makes a small man pick a fight with a big one settle scores with him. To this end he set about getting libel insurance through Tennant, Budd and Simson Ltd of Fenchurch Street in London, who eventually arranged for his policy to be underwritten by Lloyds of London. Alexander had put his insurance out to tender even though the premium was less than £20. Even with the flush of success, financial matters always had to be dealt with promptly and efficiently. Alexander read and studied contracts and argued against anything he found disagreeable. Like the engineer and quantity surveyor he had been, he realized the importance of firm foundations for any project.

With the money from his books flowing in nicely, the threat of libel (over which he probably fretted more than he should) taken care of, it was now time to spend more money and live in a more authorial style. It was also time to go back nearer to his original source of inspiration. *Song of the Earth* was already going through the process of mental fermentation which would result in the final part of the Welsh trilogy, his finest and most sustained literary achievement. One of Alexander's delights was to drive around the countryside on extended reconnaissance missions which often covered scores of miles. In the course of one such mission he had discovered a bend in the River Wye just above Chepstow where houses perched on top of a sheer limestone cliff had a spectacular view of the Welsh side, although from the vantage point of England. In 1969 Alexander, Rosina and Georgina moved to the Headlands, at Tidenham, Chepstow. It was the most expensive and best-located home they had ever occupied as a family, only The Lodge at Llanellen being comparable in terms of charm. It was at Tidenham that Alexander concluded the Welsh trilogy that had opened with *Rape of the Fair Country* and continued with *The Hosts of Rebecca*. *Song of the Earth*, the concluding volume, again published by Gollancz in July 1969 is set around Neath, Merthyr Tydfil and Aberdare, and deals with the impact of the coming of the railway on a bargee's family. The book was written in tandem with a children's book, *The White Cockade*, which at 126 pages in the 1973 paperback edition was a mere pamphlet by Cordell standards. Alexander had almost since the beginning been reviewed in the better quality newspapers and magazines. *Song of the Earth* continued in this tradition. In the *Illustrated London News* review of fiction by Dominic le Foe in the issue for 6 September 1969 the book was reviewed in the company of Stuart Cloete's *How Young They Died*, a fictionalized account of the First World War, and *Evil in a Mask* by Dennis Wheatley, who was then riding an immense wave of sales of books about the supernatural. The *Illustrated London News* was every bit as kind to Alexander as it had been to Cloete and Wheatley.

Those who know his *Rape of the Fair Country* will already have the measure of his brilliance. Set in the Hungry Forties, it is an absorbing account of life for the toiling masses – those lucky enough to be in work – in rapidly industrializing Wales. Through the measured pace of Mr Cordell's prose can be heard the thumping of the hammers, the lifting of the cage and the screams of humanity maimed, starved and poisoned by polluted water. It is not a novel of protest, it is a novel of record; the protest speaks for itself. There is a wiry vigour about the characters and the account of everyday life reads just like the account of a trained journalist.

There was a sting in the tail, though. As was often the case, Alexander was subjected to the criticism that some of his characters and situations were, to quote le Foe, 'Almost absurdly overdrawn passages of lyrical writing which I found contrived and artificial against the sterling worth of the main treatment. This is a novel compelling in its own right.' By that stage in his career, with his market well established, Alexander was able to accept that his work might not please all the critics all the time – his readership seemed more than content.

Light is thrown on an interesting side of Alexander's character by a very much briefer report in the *South Wales Argus* when *Song of the Earth* was chosen by the Literary Guild as book of the month. In west Wales Alexander had bought a caravan and according to the *Argus* had towed it to Tidenham and was working from it during the summer of 1969 while the house was being readied for occupation. Throughout his life Alexander continued to show a strong ascetic streak which harked back to his Army days. Although he enjoyed the luxuries that his literary income was able to provide he would happily resort to what he called, again from the Army, 'active service conditions'. This could mean the laying aside of normal protocol (which at mealtimes demanded napkins in silver rings) in favour of scratch meals eaten more or less on the hoof, or it could mean field research, as with the detailed survey that had preceded *Rape of the Fair Country*. Alexander was never happier than when 'out on reconnaissance' in a car with a packet of sandwiches and a flask of tea, or making a stop at a fish and chip shop. The caravan reflected this austere trait in him. Within its small confines, with just a small table and typewriter, a calor gas light and scratch meals, he was in a womb-like place ideal for creation. In a caravan he could hear the night sounds, the scuttling of small animals and the hooting of owls, and feel the pressure of the wind rocking the caravan on its wheels and hear raindrops pattering on its roof, and he was close to nature. The sounds and also the smells – bottled gas and damp woollen clothing and the slight mustiness and whiff of summers past that all caravans seem to have – seem to have inspired Alexander to write.

In 1969, after years of relative calm, British troops once more flooded the streets of Belfast, initially to protect Catholics from Protestant attack but eventually to find that those they had been protecting turned against them. The news coming out of Ireland disturbed Alexander in an artistic sense. Politically, although well to the left, Alexander never showed a flicker of interest in the contemporary Irish Republican movement, whether in its political or paramilitary manifestation. He viewed the Protestants, too, as working people. We must also remember that Alexander had been a British Army officer, a type hardly noted for its republicanism. Alexander would have seen too many deaths of men with a plain loyalty to the Crown and the Union for his feelings towards them to be compromised. He did, however, love the romantic dash of adventure that many perceive to be at the heart of Irish politics. The Welsh trilogy is seen as the centre of gravity of Alexander's work but relatively little attention is paid to the Irish trilogy (written for children) which began with *The White Cockade*, continued with *Witches' Sabbath* and in 1971 concluded with *The Healing Blade*. As shots rang out and petrol bombs were thrown on the streets of Belfast it would not have pleased the well-heeled people of Tidenham if they had known that the quiet man in their midst with the appearance and manners of an officer was writing books which showed some sympathy for the old Republican cause in Ireland.

Rosina at this time was braving her illness, encouraging Georgina in her musical development and taking the part of the model country wife. From the time of her enlistment in the Observer Corps during the war, voluntary work had been Rosina's *métier*, never more than now in the middle-class fastness of Tidenham. While Rosina was involved in a great round of tea, sandwiches and fund-raising, Alexander was dashing through the French and Irish countryside with his young hero John Regan in defence of Wolfe Tone and his plans for an invasion of Ireland. All three Irish books were published by the Viking Press in the United States where pro-Irish sentiment ran considerably higher than it did at Tidenham. Alexander may have liked the cut and dash which he perceived the Irish cause to possess but his own existence was ruled by unglamorous deadlines. During the Tidenham years several aspects of Alexander's character showed in rapid succession. He was the ascetic enjoying the simple life in the caravan which the Grabers had bought for weekends and holidays. He could be the model middle-class husband and father, and he could be, in his mind at least, the desperate revolutionary running through the countryside with the very army in which he had served hard on his heels. He also knew how to enjoy the fruits of his labours. On Christmas Eve 1969 a letter from the manager of the Chepstow branch of Lloyds Bank informed Alexander that the Bank of England had agreed to his request for some of his savings to be used to buy a car in Poland, a difficult procedure at the time due to British restrictions on the export of currency. And Ireland was on his mind for reasons quite other than literary. In August 1969 his financial advisers, Dorrell, Oliver and Co. of Abergavenny, who had been dealing with some complicated negotiations involving copyright and inheritance, concluded in a letter: 'With all these taxation complications we would think that domicile in the Irish Republic gets more attractive.' In other words, it was time for Alexander to consider becoming a tax exile.

Chapter Twelve

Given the nomadic habits of the Graber family, a relocation to Ireland, where writers paid no income tax, seemed an obvious move. Alexander, however, chose not to lead his little family into exile. Instead he had gone ahead with the purchase of the Headlands at Tidenham, using his caravan as a base for much of the time while the paperwork was completed. It was a surprising move, especially in view of the fact that the UK tax authorities were being less than accommodating. On 23 January 1970 HM Inspector of Taxes, writing from Finsbury Park in London, made it clear that the Inland Revenue intended to lay claim to a large chunk of what Alexander had received in film rights. Why did Alexander not decamp to Ireland? On the face of it, the Irish Republic had everything he was looking for. Property prices at the time were far cheaper than in Britain, income tax exemptions were mouth-wateringly attractive to a man in his financial position and, as the publication of his Irish trilogy for children had shown, there was plenty of room for literary endeavour. At that time the Roman Catholic church wielded considerable authority in matters of censorship but experienced writer that he was, Alexander could easily have steered his way around any problems of that sort, particularly as almost all his sales would be in Britain anyway.

There were two reasons for his remaining, one personal, the other literary. Wales was to remain his centre of gravity, the point to which he would always return. Ever since the Grabers had moved to 7 Holywell Crescent, which Alexander had named Ubique (in 1998 the carved wooden nameplate he had made was still on the gatepost), the friendship with Elsie May had continued unabated. On 24 August 1960 Elsie, later almost exclusively known as Donnie, had become a widow with the death of her husband. Donnie was short, only a little over five feet, with warm brown eyes and an affectionate but determined character. Much liked also by Rosina, the foursome which was now three had become close friends, so much so that Alexander would not have countenanced a move which put Donnie far beyond his reach. There was also the fact of Rosina's illness. By January 1970 Alexander was contemplating a holiday which would take him to Rome, Vienna and Warsaw and had gone so far as to ask his travel agent, Atlas Travel, of 26 High Street, Chepstow, to supply him with hotel brochures and sort out any currency problems. Such a diversion, though, could not make the fact of Rosina's illness go away, nor on the literary front could it

Tidenham, *c.*1971. One of the last pictures taken with Rosina.

sweeten the first unpleasant taste of rejection. Since *Rape of the Fair Country*'s debut it seemed that Alexander Cordell could do no wrong in the eyes of his publisher, Victor Gollancz Ltd. On 2 January 1970, however, a letter signed personally by Livia Gollancz, the publishing house's managing director, and her joint managing director politely informed Alexander that a children's book entitled 'The Spanish Slave' was not, from the Gollancz perspective anyway, up to snuff. The Gollancz letter makes it appear that there was more than one manuscript, though none now survive. As a let-down, the letter is a diplomatic masterpiece: 'I think the books are excellent of their sort; they have enormous vitality and fertility of invention and your descriptions of the motion behind the scenes of violent action grip and involve the reader,' Livia Gollancz wrote, before sweetly delivering the blow.

> But they are not the sort of books that would sit well on our children's list – indeed, we have never published anything like them and have always concentrated on rather longer books of plot and character with, wherever possible, a cleverly concealed moral. If we were to publish *The Spanish Slave* I feel we would have great difficulty in giving the book adequate promotion. The books are not the sort people expect of us, nor that our sales department have experience in selling, and I am afraid that my own lack of enthusiasm for this sort of book could not help but be transmitted to the others concerned. Please forgive me for writing a

letter that must be a disappointment to you. You know that I think the world of your books and equally you know me well enough to realize that, feeling as I do about *The Spanish Slave*, I do not wish to undertake a publication to which, I am quite sure, we could not do justice.

With several substantial books behind him, Alexander was hardly likely to be rattled by this letter, but he was disconcerted. Relationships appear to have remained cordial and Alexander could hardly have complained that Livia Gollancz's point was in any way unreasonable. A long relationship between author and publishing house was, however, over. In future, he would turn to Hodder and Stoughton, of which Coronet Books was the paperback imprint and which would appear on the spine of his next offering, *The Fire People*. As he contemplated his change of loyalties, Alexander reflected that his financial situation, at any rate, was secure. In an interview with the *South Wales Echo*, Cardiff's evening newspaper, he told a female feature writer over lunch at the George Hotel in Chepstow that he was a wealthy man who, if he did not get a £5,000 advance on a book, wanted to know what was wrong. The film rights of *Rape of the Fair Country*, he revealed, had been sold for £20,000 and Stanley Baker still intended to make the film. Truthfully, he said that money was not important to him, although he made no attempt to disguise the pleasure that spending it could bring. He pointed out that he drove a seven-year-old Ford, could not remember when he last bought a new suit and 'never went out anywhere' apart from musical concerts, yet the meal seems to have been convivial, plentifully supplied with sherry, and wine with the steaks, paid for by Alexander. He may not have bought many suits recently, but the picture which accompanied the article showed him wearing a tweed jacket of superior cut with a discreet triangle of handkerchief peeping from the breast pocket, and his hair was stylishly groomed. Later on that year, Alexander informed the firm of solicitors he had retained in Haverfordwest that Rosina wished to make her will. It was a sign of increasing pessimism, brought about by his first rejection since his early apprentice days and the fact of Rosina's failing health. The cloud that had been gathering on their horizon was becoming heavier and darker all the time. Within two years it was to engulf Alexander completely, throwing him into a pit of despair from which he would need all his courage to emerge.

If Alexander had decided against moving to Ireland for financial and personal reasons, his imagination hovered for a while in that country, which for him was both a place and a state of mind. *The Fire People* opens with one of the most exuberant passages of any of his books:

There was more commotion going on than a Tipperary bath night. Big Bonce was clogging around with Lady Godiva; Curly Hayloft, as bald as an egg, was doing a bull-fight with Tilly; Skin-Crone the cook was beating time to the shriek of the fiddle and the navvy hut was alive with the dancers of Kerry and County Mayo.

While all the wild jigging is going on Peg Jarrotty, the wake corpse, is slung in the corner with a rope under his armpits and propped up with a broom under his chin and a pint of beer slopping in his hand and gets tickled under the chin as Tilly goes dancing by. Somebody turns up the lights, and by this device Alexander introduces the details of the inside of the hut. There is a confusion of coats and blankets and muddy boots, and some twenty beds. His ingenious way of telling us the precise year and time of the year is by making Peg Jarrotty have a sign hung around his neck with his name and the county of his birth and the date of his death:14 June 1830. Several elements of Alexander's unique style are introduced straight away. In many of his books there is someone who, like Curly Hayloft, is 'as bald as an egg'. When it looks as though a brawl might erupt between the Welsh Jobina and the ebullient Tilly over the treatment of the corpse, Tilly 'breasts up' in the face of the Welsh woman, a descriptive and original use of language to describe offended female dignity.

The Fire People was published on 3 January 1972 by Hodder and Stoughton and was the first of Alexander's books to carry a decimal price, £2.25. The author had come out of his corner fighting and his new publishers showed their confidence in him by securing 20,000 orders from bookshops in advance of publication. Central to *The Fire People* is the story of Dic Penderyn, or Richard Lewis, a young miner who in 1831 was one of a deputation of iron-workers demanding the restitution of their wages following a 40 per cent cut. A fight broke out between the workers and some soldiers in which a soldier was wounded with his own bayonet. Mayhem ensued which included the discharge of firearms with many fatalities. Dic Penderyn was seized and charged with the wounding of a soldier. Having been found guilty he was hanged at Cardiff. The drama and tragedy bound up in this, one of the most significant working-class risings of the nineteenth century, are detailed by the author with a reporter's eye. His prose is as modulated as the beat of a drum, or the volleys of Highlanders' musketry. Alexander reconnoitred the book well, just as he had done with *Rape of the Fair Country,* and took pleasure in his description.

'Dic Penderyn lived in China, a part of Merthyr which was a sink of iniquity in those days', he informed Roland Chambers of the *South*

Wales Argus. 'It was a crazy, sagging, criss-crossed roofed slum of tortuous alleys and waterless, drainless cottages. It was lorded, of course, by Cyfarthfa Castle, with its eighteen beautiful acres of parkland and William Crawshay the Second, the enigmatic, efficient, meteoric, ruthless paternal ironmaster.' If there was a contradiction in being ruthless and paternalistic at the same time it did not seem to matter. His readers knew what he meant. In the right mood Alexander was an interviewer's dream with all the superb images of criss-crossed roofed slums and lashings of iniquity served up to copy-hungry journalists. Alexander had done his research well. From Tidenham he had driven to Merthyr to pace out the scene of the action and had spent much time in libraries. Mr John Collett and Mr Michael Elliott of Newport Library were both particularly helpful to him and were acknowledged, as was Mr Tom Whitney of Merthyr Tydfil Library who had shown him some maps of early nineteenth-century Merthyr. The relationship with Newport Library in particular was one which Alexander had treasured since the early days of researching *Rape of the Fair Country*. The interest generated by *The Fire People* spilled over into getting permission from Cardiff City Council to put up a plaque to the memory of Dic Penderyn at the St Mary Street entrance to Cardiff Market, no more than a few yards from where Dic Penderyn's gallows had stood. Before *The Fire People* it had been generally thought that Dic Penderyn was a scapegoat hanged simply as an example to the others. After Cordell, he is written in the pages of history books as a working-class hero. By diligent digging in Home Office files, Alexander turned up a bundle of papers relating to the case which had been filed away after Penderyn's conviction and had never since seen the light of day. Sensationally, the papers suggested that Penderyn, although known to be a leader of the Merthyr Rising, did not actually stab the soldier and that false evidence had been brought against him. The uncovering of the documents in Bundle Zp 37 of HO 17/128 part 2 were a genuine coup and a testament to the author's thoroughness.

By January 1972 the pressures upon Alexander were beginning to show. In the *South Wales Echo* of 4 January he made the first of a series of attacks on the Welsh Arts Council, which disbursed government money throughout the whole of the cultural spectrum. Even to his friends, the accusation he levelled against the Arts Council, that it spent too much money on 'petty poets' or 'two stanza poets' seemed ungenerous. In an interview following publication of *The Fire People* he told Cardiff journalists:

The Arts Council should be looking for the great Welsh novelist of the future. I am sure that when he is found he will come from the valleys, the despised valleys. I am sick to death of the Welsh Arts Council which, in my opinion, is doing nothing to project the undoubted talent and potential for novelists which exists in the Principality.

Uttered at the height of his power, this seemed very much like hauteur. From time to time, for the rest of his life, Alexander would occasionally rail against the 'official' or 'establishment' art which he felt the Arts Council espoused. An impartial observer would, of course, realize that he could not have it all ways. If the Arts Council was on the side of the Establishment, it could not simultaneously be on the side of impoverished pub poets. If it was sponsoring sometimes subversive pub poets it was hardly likely to endear itself to the Establishment. It was almost as though Alexander had decided upon an attack upon the Arts Council as a central plank of his publicity campaign. The day before his 4 January outburst in the *South Wales Argus*, he had been reported as saying:

I think there is a tremendous laziness, particularly among Welsh writers of today. They are now producing phonetic poetry with wiggle-waggle coggle wodgers and this is being broadcast, with no verse or anything at all, because of its assumed originality. Wales is again sinking into iniquity. You can dial a poem courtesy of the Welsh Arts Council – an obscene poem containing four-letter words.

It was left to Roland Chambers of the *Argus* to ask Alexander the only pertinent question there was to be asked under the circumstances, which was whether Alexander had ever received a prize from the Welsh Arts Council. 'No,' was the reply. 'One might readily wonder why. I have not received a penny, and if I had I would probably give it to charity.' The thrust of Alexander's argument, as reported by Roland Chambers, was that one should not have to be Welsh to qualify for Welsh Arts Council help (which one did not anyway). Then it seemed the argument altered course slightly and seemed to take on a more personal note. In an apparent reference to himself he said, 'I mean this seriously . . . that the Welsh Art Council's reply to this would be that he's got enough money, acumen and literary acceptance anyway so the money should go to the people who have not got this.' As a self-proclaimed socialist Alexander could hardly have been complaining about state support for the arts. Who was not worthy of support, his friends wondered, if it was not the people at the bottom of the cultural pile who nevertheless showed promise? It was a row never to be resolved. Until the end of his life Alexander and the Welsh Arts Council had a strained relationship. It also had to be said that many of his friends detected pride in the successful author's attitude. The fact that prior to this spat Alexander had approached the Welsh Arts Council with a plan to organize a novel competition named after, and adjudicated by, him, which had twice been politely rebuffed, is probably significant.

By the spring of 1972 Alexander's attentions were once more returning to China. The book which three years later was to emerge as *The Dream and the Destiny* was already forming itself in his mind. By April 1972 both theme and plot were substantially in place, much of the impetus having come from Hodder and Stoughton, who commissioned it. It was to be a tale on an epic scale, 150,000 words long, about the fighting retreat of Mao Tse Tung's Long March through the besieging forces of Chiang Kai Shek, a retreat which covered 8,000 miles across eighteen mountain ranges, and took 368 days, 235 of which were spent fighting. Given the scale of events the human possibilities were endless and the subject matter appealed very much to the soldier in Alexander. The book was not to be published for three years. In fact the Orwellian *If You Believe the Soldiers* was to reach the bookshops first.

Rosina, Alexander's wife of thirty-five years, died on 20 May 1972 at Resolven, while her husband was giving a talk. She had sat down and died of a heart attack, the culmination of many years of faltering health. Alexander was numbed as the carousel of events and places of which he and Rosina had been a part wheeled through his mind. The first impetuous meeting on the station when Alexander, the faceless young soldier, just one in hundreds of thousands, missed his train to escort her back to her father's house, the wedding and Shrewsbury and the war years, her loving support as he pecked away at his old Remington, desperate to turn himself into a writer, Georgina, the delirium with which Gollancz's acceptance of *Rape of the Fair Country* was greeted, Hong Kong, snowballing literary fame – all now seemed as ashes in his mouth. The pain of Rosina's loss was never to leave Alexander. At the Conifers, his final home at Wrexham after Donnie's death, a portrait of Rosina hung on the wall together with a picture of Donnie, over Donnie's favourite chair. He was to take a picture of Rosina with him, quite literally to his death. One brisk spring day, when the warm wind brought a promise of new life, Alexander and Georgina took Rosina's ashes up the Skirrid mountain overlooking Abergavenny and released her, to be as one with the countryside which had come to mean in-expressibly more to her than the flatness of her native south-east England. Alexander himself was fifty-seven years of age, and in the wind that pulled at the hem of his coat as he stood for a moment, bareheaded and with moist eyes, he felt intimations of his own mortality.

In the foreword to *The Haunted Holy Ground* by Mike Buckingham and Richard Frame published many years afterwards, Alexander Cordell wrote, 'We grieve, of course, and deeply, for our loved ones: I myself believe the death of a beloved wife or husband is the worst event in human life, including death by fire.' The words give us some idea of the depth of grief of the man as, with the last of the ashes being whipped away in a flurry, he turned and walked slowly back to his car. Retreat from the world was Alexander's way of dealing with his grief. The Headlands at Tidenham was put on the market for £22,300 with another £1,800 for fittings and in August he moved into a rented caravan in the Forest of Dean to mourn, and to continue work on his next book which was to be *If You Believe the Soldiers*. He also began to drink heavily, the first time in his life that he had consistently done so. During the days in his static caravan at Coleford, Alexander would write or sometimes simply mope. On dull evenings, when even the generous dimensions of the luxury caravan became claustrophobic, he would put the cover over his typewriter and drive into town for a meal or a drink. Although there was a great deal of money in the bank his voluntarily reduced circumstances fuelled the impression he had given himself that he was poor.

This was the time in his life when Alexander most closely identified with the Marxist Left, as represented by the Communist Party of Great Britain (at that time undivided, and still a considerable force within the labour and trade union movements) and the International Socialists, later to become the Socialist Workers' Party. The early 1970s were salad days for the Left, more for the small Trotskyite groupings such as the International Socialists than the Communist Party which had been tainted by Stalinism. The International Socialists also had the best weekly newspaper, the *Socialist Worker*, and it was to this paper that Alexander contributed a piece on Dic Penderyn. The lurid headline was 'Murder of a Union Man' which conveniently ignored the fact that the hanging of Dic Penderyn was a judicial execution. *If You Believe the Soldiers* casts light on Alexander's emotions and thoughts in the period following Rosina's death. Most obviously, he felt the anger at Rosina's being taken away from him. Whenever soldiers were mentioned in Alexander's books he generally made a favourable reference to the ordinary foot-soldier who, like the working man who was his brother, was the salt of the earth. *If You Believe the Soldiers* paints a bleak portrait of the army from the ordinary soldiers right up to Colonel Bull Brander, the 'new Cromwell' who rules Britain from the royal yacht *Britannia* moored in the Thames, while the Queen is a virtual prisoner in Buckingham Palace. Alexander's black vision is fed by his despair at Rosina's death. His own sense of God having failed him personally and humanity generally (he would not have put it that way) was unconsciously sketched out in the scene in which an elderly bishop is executed:

> In his long, grey gown he went, inches above the marching soldiers. He looked hard and long at the sky, I remember, as they tied him to the post and turned away his head as they offered to bandage his eyes. The bullets of the firing squad cracked raggedly through the red dawn, manipulating his thin limbs like those of a disjointed puppet in a cacophony of ricochets and he slowly sagged forward, his head on his chest, then dropped to his knees and died.

There is something of Calvary about this passage, with little psychological touches such as the reference to ricochets, which hark back to his own wounding.

At several times in his life, usually when he was experiencing the most anxiety, Alexander was to voice fears that the 'Establishment', in whichever of its manifestations, was somehow 'out to get him'. Sometimes it was the Welsh Arts Council perversely (as he saw it) withholding patronage or it could be the more tangible force of the police or secret service.

The central question of *If You Believe the Soldiers* was could such a right-wing coup of the Francoist variety happen here? Alexander's view, forged by his own pessimism and the political thinking of the Left at the time, was that it could. 'I once remember arguing with someone that Britain could never spawn such people,' he said at the time. 'I thought it was a Germanic production awaiting the mad spark of Hitlerism but the person I was talking to argued that it was the product of extremism and they (the potential oppressors) existed everywhere irrespective of dictatorship or democracy and that it only needed a leap into extremism of any kind to bring them blinking into the light.' The aim of *If You Believe the Soldiers* was to 'frighten people into action', Alexander would say, although if you were to ask him what this action might be, he would be unspecific. He did not see a left-wing popular uprising as the necessary antidote to a right-wing coup, for he told several interviewers at the time of publication: 'What it boils down to is that the classes of this country must learn to live together.' The book was a plea for tolerance rather than a call to action. 'I have set myself the task of rubbing out all class distinction by setting the ball of self-criticism rolling. If we go on as we are our future prospects are very grim indeed.'

Television pictures of Orangemen parading with Union Jacks would have gone into the mulch which was to feed his imagination and result in a book. Ireland had always fascinated Alexander and it was often linked in his memory with violence. During his boyhood he had seen two boys in the Crumlin Road in Belfast fighting with knives. The remark about 'getting the ball of self-criticism rolling' is also interesting. Mao's Cultural Revolution had set intellectuals and professional people to work in the fields so that they might share the tribulations of the rural poor. Such people were routinely expected to denounce their own shortcomings, the expected result being humility and a willingness to subsume one's efforts in the fight for the common good. A later generation would see this as coercive and as right-wing as anything Alexander might put in his books, but the author saw it as a jolly good thing in a Baden-Powellish sort of a way.

Georgina, the Grabers' only daughter, had long since gone to live in Finland, having in 1971 married Erkki Korhonen, a native of that country and at the time of their meeting a dental student. Georgina had met Erkki while working as a private English tutor for the family of a girl about her own age at Jyvaskla, a small lakeside town. She had travelled to Jyvaskla in July 1970 and met Erkki after a fortnight through the girl she was teaching, who was going out with Erkki's brother. The young couple only had three weeks initially to enjoy each other's company before Georgina had to return to Britain. The marriage was at Abergavenny with the reception at the Angel Hotel, and at the end of it Alexander and Rosina had said farewell to their daughter as she went off to make a new life in Finland. With the death of Rosina it was for Alexander to make the same, but much sadder, journey. Towing his touring caravan across northern Europe, he delivered the household effects Rosina wanted their daughter to have.

Back in Britain, as the sale of the Tidenham house went ahead and Alexander alternately worked and brooded in his rented caravan, the old travelling impulse became stronger and he stepped up his plans to go to China. In September 1972, in order to research *The Dream and the Destiny*, Alexander flew to China and immediately upon arriving wrote a letter to Elsie Donovan, his Abergavenny neighbour. Three

117

letters were sent back to the United Kingdom in as many days. Alexander had suffered, had gone into retreat and now, inspired by China which always seemed to have an effect upon him, he had come to a decision. He would ask Elsie Donovan, widowed twelve years before and the friend of both himself and Rosina since the time they moved into Holywell Crescent, to be his housekeeper. This intention may have been formed as early as September, when the letters from Hong Kong began. Concrete steps had been taken by January 1973. On 4 January Price and Son, his Haverfordwest solicitors, acknowledged receipt of a cheque for £5,400 against the purchase of 'Afallon', Waen Wen, Glasinfryn, near Bangor in north Wales, with occupation as from 1 February. The first months of 1972, with *The Fire People* in print and *If You Believe the Soldiers* already in draft form, represent a very creative period of Alexander Cordell's life and yet just as in an air journey when one senses, rather than feels, that the pilot is nearing his destination and is beginning to descend, there were the very first intimations of an ending.

The death of Rosina had, of course, delivered a wounding blow and, in his fifty-eighth year and with thirteen books behind him, the old soldier was tiring. He was becoming querulous, something that was to happen increasingly when he was under stress. The first instance of this had been a row concerning some fittings for the rented caravan which, on his part, was litigious bordering on the cranky. The seventeen-foot caravan which was his home during the leaving of Tidenham and the move to north Wales was not new but was of high quality and in good condition and luxuriously appointed by the standards of the day with many extra fittings, including an Electrolux refrigerator. When the refrigerator began to go wrong Alexander immediately contacted his lawyers and insisted they begin a correspondence with the caravan's suppliers. Impatiently, Alexander had the appliance repaired at his own cost, the bill coming to £9.12, even in 1973 hardly a king's ransom. But in the most aggrieved terms Alexander wrote to Price and Son demanding that the suppliers, who had been slow to recompense him, be pressed into payment. There was also the smaller matter of a broken car-caravan mirror. Price and Sons' initial enquiries seemed to suggest that the suppliers felt the fault was not all theirs and that Alexander might have to prepare himself for legal action.

In mid-February the law firm delivered what can only be seen as a polite rebuke. Any action against the company, Pearman Briggs, for the cost of the repair would be fraught with difficulty, he was told, since the company had offered to buy a new refrigerator and install it in the

Wedding day, 1973, Bangor. With Georgina.

caravan at no cost to Alexander, an offer which he had rejected. He was advised that, as he had failed to give the company an opportunity of repairing the defective refrigerator under guarantee, the matter should be abandoned after one further letter.

Several days later Price and Son again wrote to Alexander telling him that a cheque had been received in his favour for £10.22. A man with tens of thousands of pounds in the bank and an expectation of very much more had expended nervous energy he could not spare over the price of a good meal for two. Price and Son were rarely out of correspondence in these months over other matters and the subject of a great proportion of this flurry of paperwork was Donnie. In the months since Rosina's death the deep affection Alexander had always felt for Donnie took a more intimate direction. It was certainly tactful, to avoid any taint of scandal, to take up residence in north Wales where details of the friendship between Alexander and Rosina and Donnie were not known. The official 'line' was that Donnie was to join Alexander at Glasinfryn as his housekeeper, but the fact of the matter was that marriage was the aim. On 31 May 1973 the couple were indeed married. Alexander triumphantly changed the name of his house to 'Fair Country' and a new life was commenced at a discreet distance from south Wales. Alexander grew a beard, despite his oft-repeated disapproval of anything more luxuriant than the military moustache he had always sported. Psychologists might well read into this an unconscious attempt to hide his identity or in some way cover his tracks. They would be right. At about this time Alexander issued instructions to his publishers that any biographical notes issued were to be brief. The consummate showman was now disinclined to draw attention to himself.

The querulous mood displayed in the matter of the caravan had still not been dispelled by the summer of 1973 when Alexander appears to have had reservations about Bookwise, distributors of *The Fire People* for Coronet Books. The matter, in which Coronet had increasingly to defend Bookwise, rumbled on like a distant thunderstorm all through the summer. The air was heavy with barely restrained feelings between Alexander and Coronet and continued to crackle with electricity until 4 July when the storm broke. Ron Read, who was handling the matter for Coronet, first placated the author by saying that he had good reason to be upset at the poor showing *The Fire People* was making in Bookwise outlets. After more vociferous complaints from Alexander, Ron Read felt compelled to write a letter which was slightly sharper in tone, imploring Alexander to let Bookwise make amends by improving distribution so that his book would be 'available for everyone in Wales to read', and not to let this problem get out of proportion. The required submission was not tendered. A letter fired off from Read on 1 August was short and sharp.

> I was sorry to see in your letter of July 16 that there was still some feeling about Bookwise. This was confirmed to me the other day when I heard that you had written another letter to Alan Thomas, the Bookwise area manager, about your visit to a Woolworth's branch in his area. Frankly Alex, you are not helping the situation by writing such letters and I am finding it increasingly difficult to maintain the goodwill and the display space we have so far enjoyed for your books. I am very anxious to resolve the situation to the outcome [*sic*] of everyone concerned and I hope that a meeting [between the area manager and others and Alexander] in Liverpool on Friday, August 10 will provide an opportunity to restore harmonious relations all round.

Five days later, which was four days before the Liverpool meeting, Read wrote another letter suggesting that Bookwise had been 'unduly sensitive' in its dealings with Alexander. Although properly attending to his interests, it seemed that once more Alexander's insistence had inflamed rather than helped resolve a situation at a time when the mental effort was really required for other things.

If You Believe the Soldiers, published in August 1973, got off to a slow start, despite considerable efforts put into its launch by Hodder and Stoughton, and particularly Eric Major of that company. Newspapers solicited for reviews included *The Times*, the *Guardian*, the *Observer*, the *Sunday Telegraph*, the *Daily Telegraph*, the *Scotsman*, the *Evening Standard*, the *Irish Times*, the *Glasgow Herald*, the *Yorkshire Post* and the *Liverpool Daily Post*. In the second barrage of ranging shots aimed at the smaller dailies, the *South Wales Argus* led the list with a copy sent to Ken Griffin, then the editor, the *South Wales Evening Post*, with two copies to the *Western Mail* and the *South Wales Echo*. A handful of MPs – including Roy Hughes, Newport East, and Roy Hattersley were included as were two newspapers representing bitter enemies – the *Morning Star*, allied to what was in those days, before the doctrinal split the Communist Party of Great Britain, and the *Socialist Worker*. The review by Eddie Woods in the *Morning Star* was a classic of the period. Headlined '1984 – but not as Orwell imagined', the article spoke of Alexander Cordell's 'imaginative idea' of where the 'obscene' policies of Edward Heath's government, which in 1973 was in power, might lead. The implementation of Powellite 'racist' measures and the 'barbarities' of Northern Ireland were seen as having fascism as their corollary, an assumption that was common at the time. With the wisdom of hindsight, we may permit ourselves a smile at Mr Woods's, prognosis. *If You Believe the Soldiers* was taken seriously by the Left. At that year's Labour Party Conference at Blackpool Maurice Edelman, Roy Jones and Eric Heffer were all seen clutching copies.

As the 1970s came to a close Alexander was in the mood for sustained writing. *To Slay the Dreamer* (1980) and *Rogue's March* were begun at about the same time. As early as October 1979 the author was writing to the museum of the Welch Regiment in Cardiff asking for precise details of the procedure when a man was drummed out of a British Army regiment. The reply was prompt – it was one of the occasions upon which he found his military rank to be useful. The request is indicative of the thoroughness with which Alexander always conducted his research. The information might be readily obtainable from reference books, but for him it had to come 'straight from the horse's mouth'.

Rogue's March is one of the most interesting of Alexander's works, not particularly for its style or content but for the degree to which Alexander identified with its hero, James Alexander McAndrew (note the middle name). McAndrew was the man who was drummed out of the Army for desertion and must stand as one of the most obnoxious characters ever to be given life by the author. A rapist and cheat, the psychopathic McAndrew was a massive Scotsman who would inflict pain without remorse and yet weep at the trilling of birds or at the sight of flowers. Alexander's fondness for the character was unaccountable to many, but the character of McAndrew contained many of the traits of his creator, though writ large. Alexander always admired prowess in fighting, and while his own attitude to women was never less than courteous, he always had a sneaking admiration for any man who was a 'broth of a boy'. Much of the sensitivity in the book is Alexander's but it is rarely expressed by McAndrew and when it is it takes the form of a treacly sentimentality. The real compassion, as so often is the case, is expressed by the women.

The 1970s were a decade in which the former Army major with the precise manners had become firmly identified with the Left in politics. He had once been a member of the Anglo-Rhodesian Society (for reasons now far beyond anyone's recall) but had resigned at the time of Rhodesian premier Ian Smith's unilateral declaration of independence. The stiff letter from the society formally accepting his resignation is unintentionally amusing. From a Miss B. A. Williams it reads:

> I refer to your letter of the 8th of September and am rather amazed at your comments. What is it that has so appalled you? I wonder what it was you saw in Rhodesia and to whom did you speak. With respect, if you have travelled through Southern Africa you could not have failed to see how well-off and more content the black Rhodesian is in comparison with his Northern brothers.

One hopes, for the sake of Rhodesia, or Zimbabwe as it now is, that Miss Williams's idiosyncratic prose did not penetrate high levels in that country's administration.

Given Alexander's general appearance, it is also amusing to see him as a 'soul brother' but that is exactly what he was to the black inmates of Marion Federal Penitentiary in Illinois, USA. On behalf of the Black Culture Society within the prison Mr Kamau na Mwando (aka Gordon L. Faust), public relations officer for the BCS, sent Alexander a letter asking for any complimentary or damaged copies he may have had of

The Dream and the Destiny, 'which, we assure you, will be treasured by these, your incarcerated brothers'. It was signed 'In ideological clarity, Kamau na Mwando'. The letter was meticulously polite and well presented despite having come from a representative (Marion being a federal gaol) of some pretty tough and desperate characters. Kamau na Mwando, to give Mr Faust his African name, seems to have turned the prison into a Marxist-Leninist university and adopted Alexander as some sort of emeritus don.

Chapter Thirteen

Alexander and Donnie had discreetly slipped their moorings at Bangor and moved to the Isle of Man during the 1970s to take up residence at Rebecca, 130 Friary Park, Ballabeg, Castletown. It was here that *To Slay the Dreamer*, Alexander's book about the Spanish Civil War, was completed. By Cordell standards *To Slay The Dreamer* was a rushed job and, although the action is centred on the city of Avila, during his Spanish visit he only once left Barcelona, many kilometres distant, and that was for a visit to the Pyrenees. It was while in the mountains that he became caught in a torrential storm so fierce that he feared for his life. The original plan had been to include Pamplona in the itinerary but he had heard of a Fascist rally to be held in the city and had decided that Donnie should remain safely at home.

Shortly after he returned home, negotiations over the possible filming or televising of *Rape of the Fair Country* reopened. Many years before Alexander had sold the film rights of the book to John Barnes Productions Inc. of Brooklyn Heights, New York, USA. Several attempts had been made to render the book in visual form, but all had come to naught. The 1980s opened with a renewed spate of interest from John Barnes, who had corresponded with Alexander on and off since the 1960s. The spring of 1980 had seen HTV nibbling at the bait that had been dangling for some years a televised version of *Rape of the Fair Country*. Patrick Dromgoole, for the Welsh television channel, wrote to Alexander asking to meet him on the Isle of Man but in July cancelled by telegram, pleading pressing commitments. John Barnes had already written a television script and could hardly have been disappointed when BBC Wales started to take an interest. In the December, Alexander received an excited letter from Barnes saying that the BBC had taken up an option on a television production. The letter dispatched from Barnes's home in Brooklyn Heights raised Alexander's hopes to a new level. As the year closed, nothing seemed more certain than that *Rape of the Fair Country* would at last appear on the small screen. 'The deed is done,' John Barnes wrote. 'I have signed the contract with the BBC . . . it is all set . . . after all these years of frustration – yours longer than mine – it's to come alive on the screen. I wish we could drink together.' This enthusiasm was initially shared by Alexander but his mood swung to one of the deepest scepticism once the television script was in his hands and had been read. A letter to BBC producer John Gethin in July 1981 made this disappointment clear. It was, he fumed,

Barcelona, 1974, while researching *To Slay the Dreamer*.

a harsh copy of *How Green Was My Valley* and something vital will have to be done to bring it onto the international rails . . . I am appalled by the necessity for the Welsh to sing at every opportunity . . . the Welsh sing, if pressed to, at weddings, but prefer funerals. Drunk, they will sing their hearts out and at rugby matches if they think they are going to win.

At this time Alexander was going through one of his periodic bouts of pessimism as to the capacity of the Welsh working class to bring about radical change. A slight but noticeable retreat from his hitherto incandescent enthusiasm for Wales and all things Welsh is signalled by his mentioning to John Barnes that he would sooner not have a Welsh director for the televised version of *Rape of the Fair Country*. 'I don't trust Welsh directors. Somewhere lurking behind the gregarious exterior is usually a chapel fiend swimming in the River Jordan. Under stress they are inclined to return to the Band of Hope of their omnipresent childhood.'

In December 1981 John Barnes wrote to Alexander saying he was becoming frustrated at the project's apparent lack of progress, and by the middle of 1982 it was depressingly clear to all parties that the deal was becoming unpicked at the seams. By this time Alexander had made his reservations about the television script known to John Barnes, bringing the relations between the two men to a low ebb. Under the circumstances it was generous of John Barnes to offer to sell the film rights of *Rape of the Fair Country* back to Alexander at the same price he had paid for them in the 1960s. Alexander never took up the offer. By 1983 the floundering project was finally abandoned when the BBC announced that its budget could no longer stretch to so lavish a production. Although there is no suggestion that Alexander was feeling the pinch financially – he was at the height of his earning powers – his essential frugality showed through in November 1981 when he offered thirteen of his original manuscripts, including *This Sweet and Bitter Earth*, *The Fire People*, *Rogue's March*, *The Dream and the Destiny* and *To Slay The Dreamer,* to the special collections department of Boston University. In correspondence with Dr Howard B. Gotlieb, director of special collections, who had already acquired the manuscript of *The Sinews of Love*, *The White Cockade* and *Race of the Tiger,* Alexander stuck out for $500 per manuscript, with another $500 for the manuscripts of several of the short stories dating back to the 1940s. Even at that time these earnings from the sale of the manuscripts did not amount to a great deal. Their sale merely underlines Alexander's basic asceticism. Although his homes were comfortable, and sometimes quite luxurious, one always had the feeling that he was camping in them; that his presence was transitory. The manuscripts were merely possessions to be disposed of in some preferably beneficial fashion. The soldier, who must carry all his possessions around in his kit-bag, still lurked within.

Another thing that Alexander seemed to be leaving behind was his brief interest in the sectional politics of the Left. From the end of 1980 and the beginning of 1981 he was courted by an organization calling itself 'The Hosts of Rebecca' under the leadership of Paddy French. As is often the case, the Hosts were in the process of starting a fighting fund. Mr French, in a letter dated 21 January 1981 pronounced himself delighted that he had received a donation from a man living in a house named Rebecca, 'and from the man who brought the name back to life in modern times'. Mr French's solicitations, as well as for money, were for contributions to a magazine. A fluent writer, with a cogent view of what was required, Mr French wanted Alexander to contribute to a section of the magazine which was provisionally entitled 'Flashback' in which writers and historians would discuss their technique. Alexander was obviously touched by Mr French's sincerity and commitment and replied, setting out some of his own attitudes to his work in detail. His first point, though, was to answer sporadic criticism that he had exiled himself on the Isle of Man for tax reasons. 'I'm not anything like as rich as some make out, and I'm here (of course, it's an old cry) because initially I wanted to write a trilogy of children's books on the island, not for tax purposes: we stayed mainly because we wanted to get away from it all – what chance has a writer got on the mainland?'

However, though he promised to help *Rebecca* as often as he could financially, 'I wouldn't want to be involved with it because at my great age [he was 66] I have to dispense with everything that detracts from the writing of books and I still have a few more to write'. He did, however, venture the observation that cold reportage of facts lifted from the historian the vital responsibility of taking a side and diluted the impact of the reading:

> The scream of the child trapped underground. Christ – surely she shouldn't be there? . . . and why should not the accurately reporting historian take sides? Do you not have to be there to know the shock of a furnace scald or the pain of a woman in labour? Husbands themselves would be better history-makers if they were forced, en masse, to sit at women's bedsides. The crushed hand (I can see the bored faces of a hundred historians) is yours, not the possession of a dry-as-dust recorder; one gets the same sort of reaction from a bloody computer.

The passage veers towards the obscure at several points but there is no doubt that it is a reasonable account of Alexander's view of history. Mr French could have cleaned the article up with judicious use of a blue pencil and with Alexander's permission used it in the magazine. Observant readers who were also readers of Alexander's work would have noticed once again the insistence upon the female and the dwelling upon female themes, in this case childbirth. It is a little girl that is crying underground, and the references to men, even though they are presumably the sort of manual workers of whom Alexander greatly approves, are written in mildly reproving terms.

The indefinable feeling of the beginning of the end of things, age's first whisper in the author's ear of his declining power, is sharpened somewhat in a letter from Margaret Body at Hodder and Stoughton who had been reading the manuscript of *Land of My Fathers* and who wrote back a cheerful letter which nevertheless raised points about the structure of the book that were more than quibbles. Margaret Body was to spot what many others saw as a weakness – the way minor characters in Alexander's books could sometimes muscle in on the act and overshadow the main actors.

> Also you spend quite a bit of righteous indignation on the unequal state of the workers and the groundswell of Chartism so that I expected at the least there would be blood on the pavement outside the Westgate Hotel in Newport. But no, the story sidles down the canal to Cardiff with various alarms en route, true enough, but more to fulfill your prophetic 'Tale of Delwyn' than to connect the story with the mainstream of the age.

To emphasize that what she was really asking for was a sweeping reconsideration of the structure of the book, Margaret Body added that she did not think the matter was one for a snap answer. The detailed exposition of her points is full of such phrases as 'I can't follow the logic here at all', 'What's the point?' and 'Sorry to go on so, but this is all central to our main action and at present it doesn't stand up'. Before a cordial conclusion in Welsh and a greeting that included Donnie, Margaret Body wrote, 'I reckon I've become rather bossier and more difficult to please this time, Alex . . . I look forward to hearing what you think when you've had time to inwardly digest'.

Alexander railed at the letter and then decided to do the only thing a professional writer could do, which was to get on with the changes demanded. It was a disappointment and a blow to his pride, but there was more to come. On 26 April 1982 Mr Gotlieb of the University of Boston wrote in reply to Alexander's letter of 8 March in which he stuck out for $7,000 in total for his manuscripts. He had been trying to find the funds for the purchase but 'I cannot designate that large a portion of my budget at the present time. There is, of course, the possibility of doing it a bit later when another golden ship comes round the bend and into my harbour but I fear not right now.' Alexander seemed to accept the point but in his reply said that he felt he should further clarify the matter from his point of view, part of the clarification being that 'my work is probably coming to a close' and that he would prefer his manuscripts to rest with one institution rather than be spread between several private collectors.

A pursuit hardly typical of the Left which Alexander enjoyed on the Isle of Man was yachting. When the family had lived in Hong Kong they had had a small yacht christened Gina, in honour of Georgina. Whenever he had the chance, Alexander would take to the water. In 1997, only a couple of months before his death, while driving by some yachts moored near Conwy, Alexander looked out of the car window and said wistfully: 'I love messing about in boats. We [Donnie and he] discovered the Isle of Man while out on a cruise.' He never spoke of his water-borne prowess and there were never any yachting mementoes in the house but it is certain that he was fond of getting away from it all on some friend's boat, even to the point of overnight stays on board. Writing, boating and living the quiet domestic life at Ballabeg, Alexander must have felt the need to keep in touch with Wales, which he did by offering to write features on a variety of subjects for the *Western Mail* and the *South Wales Echo*. The fact that the two newspapers shared the same building and the same management worried him not at all. In June 1982 Geoffrey Rich, the *Echo*'s editor, gently ribbed Alexander for dealing with the *Western Mail*, which was technically his newspaper's rival. Alexander was researching *Peerless Jim*, the story of the Welsh-born boxer James Driscoll, and had asked the *Echo* to go through its file for cuttings. As she complied with this the librarian discovered that the *Western Mail* had already been asked to do the same thing. 'You're not in the least fussy about your friends, are you?' Rich joked. Actually, Alexander was only being his thorough self. In search of quite a minor piece of information about the *Mauretania* upon which Driscoll had apparently sailed, he had taken the trouble to write to P&O shipping line which had directed him to the Cunard Company which had actually owned the ship, Liverpool University and the Public Records Office in London.

A heartening thing for Alexander was that he was still getting admiring letters from readers who thought he could do no wrong. One letter which he kept was evidently from an employee of Gwynedd County Council, for it was written on the headed notepaper of that authority. The writer, who signed her Christian name with a circumflex over it, was presumably a Welsh-speaker and must have known

Alexander was English, castigated the English for 'sacrificing the people, anywhere in the world, for the sake of profit'. Nevertheless, the Anglophobe admitted that the Welsh, although 'aurally aware' were 'visually destitute' and abandoned their countryside to dereliction and litter. 'It is the English immigrants who are taking the lead to protect their adopted homeland.' It would have been hard for Alexander to disagree with that. The groundswell of public approbation – even if he was no longer the 'blue-eyed boy' of the publishers – was mighty. In January the Urdd (Welsh League of Youth) National Eisteddfod wrote to Alexander asking him to donate some small personal possession for a VIP raffle to which he replied by sending a signed copy of *Land of My Fathers*. To be accepted by such diligent guardians of Welsh culture was a rare honour for a non-Welsh-speaking Englishman.

Radio was a natural medium for Alexander who had a rich yet crisp accent, never faltered, and could be relied upon to come out with a colourful phrase. In January 1983 he agreed to go on Radio 4's popular *Bookshelf* programme which paid for his flight to and from the Isle of Man and a couple of pleasant days pottering in London. One of his appointments while in town was to talk to Peter Grosvenor of the *Daily Express*. The stay was expanded to three days and included a trip to Cardiff to publicize *Land of My Fathers*. Alexander was researching *To Slay the Dreamer*, his book about the Spanish Civil War, at Douglas's town library when he asked John Bowring, the borough's librarian, for help. A strong friendship grew up between them which later included Donnie and John's wife, Sue. Like the Grabers, the Bowrings were 'overcomers' from the mainland and not yet assimilated into the life of the island. 'People could be a bit suspicious of overcomers until they had been on the island about ten years and they became "stayovers". Ballabeg is a village with a church, a chapel and a shop and Alexander's home was a new place on a small estate, an utterly unexceptional house,' John Bowring said in 1998. As the friendship progressed, John and Sue would be entertained by the Grabers who lived quietly.

> I can't remember his actually having a boat although he may have been taken out by others. Most of the time he just kept on quietly with his writing. I think he was a bit worried about the introduction of the public lending right [a scheme not universally welcomed by authors by means of which they are recompensed for library loans] and he was also worried about Donnie having enough money in her old age. Their life was very unostentatious. The house was nice but I think it was mainly Donnie who took care of it. Alexander wasn't the sort of person to take

too much notice of his surroundings as long as he was free to write. I knew he was very left-wing but he didn't talk about politics a great deal. He had enormous sympathy for the working man, particularly the Welsh working class, and by extension for other workers including those of Spain who were to appear in *To Slay The Dreamer*.

The issue of whether Alexander had gone to the island to escape punitive mainland taxation was never seriously gone into, John Bowring recalls. 'He would say he didn't come to the island for tax reasons although for the past thirty years taxation has been behind almost all migration, especially by the over-50s. The Manx tend to be a bit cynical in such cases. If people say they have not come to the island for tax reasons they are usually not believed.' Publishers are by no means compelled to buy a book once it has been written, a fact of which Alexander was very well aware. Even though matters relating to income tax may not have been his chief worry in the mid-1980s there was every reason why he should seek to pay as little as possible. Instructions to his solicitors, who were compiling a new will at this time, include a list of twenty-four people who were each to receive the sum of £1,000 from his estate in the event of his death apart from two who were to receive £750. One friend was to receive £2,000, with the single largest bequest apart from Donnie – £5,000 – going to Georgina who was also to receive £15,243 in Irish Punts held in an account with the Bank of Ireland. In addition some £15,000 was held in a Post Office savings account for the immediate convenience of Donnie should Alexander die before her. Since the house in Ballabeg was valued at approximately £40,000 it meant that Alexander was worth about £100,000 at 1983 prices. It was a very substantial sum and for a man on the eve of his seventieth birthday would easily have allowed him to live the rest of his life in comfort. Still, careful husbandry was required if friends and family were to benefit to the extent he had in mind. One little quirk was £1,000 left to Tidenham Old Folks' Club to finance an annual event to be known as Rosina's Outing. This money was gratefully received and the outing was still being enjoyed in 1998.

The Bowrings were to be among the few friends the Grabers made on the island. 'There was a teacher, Ian Stuart, with whom he was friendly and an ordinary working man who was, I think, a scaffolder. Generally, though, he kept his life in separate compartments, so one set of friends did not necessarily know of the existence of others.' Mr Bowring agreed that there was something transitory about Alexander's life, a sense that he camped in any one location, rather than actually lived there. He and Sue remained friends with Alexander and Donnie and later visited them at Wrexham, their final home, and he noticed the same sense of impermanence there as he had at Ballabeg. One is perhaps reminded of a stanza of the *Rubáiyát of Omar Khayyám*, Alexander's favourite work. ''Tis but a tent where one takes his one day's rest. A sultan to the realm of Death addest; The sultan rises, and the dark Ferrash Strikes, and prepares it for another guest.' In June 1987, with hardly a word, Alexander put his house 'Rebecca' on the market and left the island. His leaving was precipitous. 'One minute he was here and the next he had gone without warning,' John Bowring recalls. Like some caravanner Alexander had struck his tent and made off in the night.

Part 4: 1987–1997

Chapter Fourteen

The first part of the 1980s had seen a paperstorm of letters between Alexander and various publishers as he sought to renegotiate deals relating to several of his books. In some of the correspondence from his agents, David Higham Associates of London, frustration with Alexander's approach going back many years is apparent. In April 1983 Bruce Hunter of Higham wrote to Alexander saying that the publishers Heinemann had liked a synopsis that had been forwarded to them and that Higham had asked for a deal between Heinemann and Pan. He reported that Pan did not want to publish Alexander's work again since they were 'a bit sore' about Alexander leaving them for Coronet all those years before. Such squabbles were increasingly part of everyday life for Alexander. The pugnacity he had shown as a young man was now sublimated into a hard-nosed attitude towards publishers. So labyrinthine could these dealings become that they consumed much of the effort Alexander should have been putting into his creative work. In the midst of the flurry of paperwork Alexander wrote to Miss Elizabeth Stevens of Curtis Brown in London, who were also representing him, to explain that he had asked Gollancz to retrieve *Race of the Tiger* from Hodder and Stoughton. He was, he said, writing the screenplay to *Race* and 'would shortly finish it'. A few days later, Alexander received news that Hodder's rights had indeed reverted to Gollancz, the publishers who had launched him to success all those years before with *Rape of the Fair Country* and for whom he always retained an affection.

In April 1983 Alexander received a letter from Mr Chris Barber, of Llanfoist, near Abergavenny, a local historian who had also written a couple of books of Gwent interest that had found a brisk sale. He asked permission to include some twenty paragraphs of *Rape of the Fair Country* plus some pictures in a local guide book provisionally entitled 'In the Footsteps of Iestyn Mortymer'. 'Such a book would not only be of special interest to people visiting Abergavenny and its residents but it would also encourage greater sales of your novel,' Barber wrote. Permission was granted and *Cordell Country* was one of the first publications of Chris Barber's Blorenge Books. Several months after Alexander's death in 1997, Barber secured the rights to reprint

Rape of the Fair Country and, in December 1998, *The Hosts of Rebecca*.

By August Alexander was beginning to feel intimations of literary mortality. He had outlined a book about navvies, the tough foot-soldiers of the Industrial Revolution who had dug the canals and laid the railways and who in historical terms lay exactly in Cordell's line of country. Bruce Hunter of David Higham Associates put the idea for a book to be provisionally entitled 'The Navvies' up to Allen Lane/ Penguin but that publishing house rejected it. Hunter wrote to Alexander with the bad news, the reply to which oozed with despair. 'Bad news from Penguin. I think the word has got around, and I am sorry that nothing has come of all your good efforts on my behalf,' Alexander mournfully typed. 'Perhaps the thing for me now is to go into purdah for a little while until the realization sinks in that I'm not really wanted. We may like *The Navvies*, but if we can't find anyone remotely interested now it can be assumed that a year's hard work on research and writing could well be wasted. In the name of posterity will you please return the synopsis to me?' The depression which set in during the middle months of 1983 was to revisit him frequently. Back in the early 1960s, when Alexander had told journalists that his next book would be his last, it was with the jaunty air of a fairground showman barking up his wares. Now came a feeling that his inspiration and increasingly his audience were forsaking him. With *Rape of the Fair Country* he had written one of the greatest novels to come out of Wales in modern times and he had written a dozen since. Could the magic touch be deserting him? It was a depressing thought. In this welter of uncertainty one truth shone through. He must continue to write. Writing was a symbol of his virility, a large part of his reason for being. He must fight on even though, at seventy years of age, he was beginning to feel that both his body and his muse were somehow conspiring against him.

Battling was in Alexander's nature. As times got tougher, his thoughts turned towards a man who had slugged it out in the ring, Peerless Jim Driscoll. Long after boxing had become unfashionable as politically incorrect, Alexander continued to love the Noble Art of which he had a considerable knowledge. For him, fighters were the last great individualists, mercenaries who hired themselves out for bloody individual combat. Hard men themselves, they often showed gentleness, generosity and restraint out of the ring. They had in fact, all the qualities he admired and wished to cultivate. In many ways the life of a boxer was not unlike that of writer. Like a boxer entering a ring, a writer when he sits behind his typewriter is utterly alone. The story of Peerless Jim Driscoll was to be a labour of love and Alexander's swan-song, or so he told Meic Stephens, editor of *The Oxford Companion to the Literature of Wales* which in August 1983 was in the process of compilation. Meic Stephens had sent a draft copy of Alexander's intended entry for comment purely as a matter of courtesy. 'Herewith the amended draft; it includes another four books not mentioned,' Alexander wrote back. 'I think "highly romanticised" is over the top but by all means put it in if you would like to. The effect will be dilution. I include *Peerless Jim* because it is now with the printers as Hodder will substantiate, and because it was my final novel it will bring the *Companion* into date.' For the umpteenth time Alexander was announcing that his current novel would be his last but this time it looked as though he might mean it.

As was often the case, upsets in his professional life sparked off changes in his private and financial life. Yet again Alexander changed his will, excising from it a friend on the Isle of Man who had formerly been his executor. There was nothing personal in this. It was merely a reflection of his creeping pessimism. Some authors drink or take drugs to kick-start tardy creative juices. Alexander's medicine to get him out of the doldrums was travel. In the summer of 1983 Alexander received an invitation from the Chinese Writers' Association to pay a three-week visit to their country accompanied by Donnie, an invitation which he accepted with some alacrity.

The letter to Meic Stephens amending the intended *Companion* entry made reference to Alexander as an 'author and broadcaster'. While the first claim was undoubtedly true, the second was somewhat tenuous since Alexander had not at that time, nor did he ever have, a substantial part of his work performed via the electronic media. As gloom increased on the publishing front, though, Alexander turned to writing scripts of his own work for film and television, something he was never particularly good at.

It was not because he lacked writing skills that his scripts were unsuccessful, but rather that he saw prospective films and plays based on his work as tributes to his own literary skills and wanted them placed in an epic frame. Even though Britain was floundering in reces-sion, his mind's eye visualized films with casts of hundreds which no producer could possibly afford and which in any case, at a time of changing fashions, few would consider necessary to get the story across. In this respect Alexander was a creature of his age, his mind fixed on the block-buster epics such as *Ben Hur* which had filled the

At the Great Wall of China with Donnie, July 1983.

screens in his own early days as a writer. As the pared-down 1980s progressed the fashion grew for small casts and condensed plots with often quite minimal stage furniture. Re-creations of whole ironworks requiring the taking over of whole towns with legions of extras was beyond most pockets by the mid-1980s and was to remain so in the following decade. Alexander's endeavours as a scriptwriter were received more with tolerance than with enthusiasm, although John Rush of David Higham allowed some exasperation to show through when he wrote to Alexander in October 1983 acknowledging receipt of an adaptation of *Rogue's March* which had been published as a book in

1981. The work 'showed promise', Rush carefully said, adding, 'in many ways it may be a little easier to find a producer as it's probably less expensive . . . as I said when we spoke on September 30 I've been truly excited by your ability to adapt your own work for television'. And then came the rebuke. 'You have, however, given me three major adaptations within a few months and I do think you should now give me time in which to see whether I can find a producer before you can adapt anything more.' A month later Curtis Brown, his other agents, also wrote to Alexander with less than good news. The continuing saga of a television adaptation of *Rape of the Fair Country* for BBC Wales had stalled once more with no immediate prospect of getting started again. Alexander and Donnie were still living on the Isle of Man at this time. As each of the depressing letters was solemnly filed away, it seemed to Alexander that events were slipping away from him and it was time to leave his island sanctuary. All his life Alexander had something of the showman about him and he was to retain this to the end. It was therefore a measure of his increasing mood of self-doubt that he refused a request by HTV Wales to appear on a chat show in Cardiff. When the lights came on and the cameras turned he usually sparkled and charmed. The HTV show would have increased his audience profile in south Wales, his traditional hunting ground. In the year of his seventieth birthday the author who delighted in rumbustious, two-fisted, swaggering heroes had become their antithesis, an old man left to bewail his declining powers.

By February 1984 the television script for *Peerless Jim* had been rejected by BBC Birmingham, BBC Wales, BBC TV, Thames Television and three independent producers. The script for *Race of the Tiger* submitted to potential producers at the same time had been rejected by Granada, Thames TV, BBC and three independent producers and *Rogue's March* had been sent back with a polite accompanying letter by the BBC, Granada and an independent. It was a long and depressing list but by the time it had trailed to its wearisome end Alexander was back in fighting mood, the pendulum of his despair having swung back towards high hopes. *To Slay the Dreamer*, which dealt with the Spanish Civil War, was now the book upon which he pinned his greatest hopes, though for the moment, the forthcoming launch of *Peerless Jim* occupied his mind. Both the *Western Mail* and its stablemate the *South Wales Echo* were bidding for serialization of the book and there was a launch party to look forward to at the Royal Oak in Cardiff, an old boxers' pub run by a descendant of Jim Driscoll. The *Echo* paid £400 for the serial rights of *Peerless Jim* in addition to purchasing several feature articles to be published in the run-up to serialization. This was small beer compared with what had gone before, when it seemed that Alexander's pen had been dipped in ambrosia, but the money was welcome enough and in the same year (1984) it was supplemented by the sale of more manuscripts to the University of Boston.

A perceptible rise in his confidence led to contact being re-established with Gollancz, publishers of *Rape of the Fair Country*. In high hopes Alexander sent off the manuscript of a work entitled 'Women Not Their Wives'. The letter back was polite, but firm. After reading the first chapter Livia Gollancz said, 'I feel rather less enthusiastic about the whole project. I do not know quite why, and it is a gut reaction, but I feel I ought to be guided by it.' Neither was the news from David Higham Associates any better. Bruce Hunter wrote to Alexander again on 18 January 1985 to say that he was still trying to sell the idea of a novel provisionally entitled 'Princess' about China and suggesting that Alexander meet Rosemary Cheetham at Century. At the same time he warned Alexander that the days when he could expect his work to be commissioned, with a fat advance, were long past: publishers were not keen to commission the next Cordell on the basis of his name alone. The meeting with Rosemary Cheetham seems not to have been a success. Alexander's stock may have been quite low with publishers but in south Wales, and in Gwent in particular, he was still revered. The income from his literary work had slowed if not to a trickle, at least to a series of spurts, but that was between him and his bank manager. As far as the public was concerned, Alexander Cordell's books were constantly on the bookshelves, new ones seemed to be coming out with acceptable frequency and old ones were being reprinted. The Old Man of Welsh Fiction could do no wrong.

By 1987 Coronet had published *The Fire People*, *Land of my Fathers* and *This Sweet and Bitter Earth* as a substantial-looking paperback trilogy. At the invitation of Chepstow Civic Society, Alexander unveiled a plaque in May 1985 near the spot from which the boat taking leading Chartists into exile had sailed. The high esteem in which Alexander was held locally if not in publishing circles, and his genuine love for local people, certainly contributed to his decision to return to Wales and did much to bolster his flagging confidence.

A letter from John Barnes in Brooklyn Heights dated 17 May 1985, in reply to one from Alexander asking if he should submit his script of *Rape of the Fair Country* to the BBC, put things plainly. John Barnes, who held the film and play rights told Alexander that writing scene-by-scene transcriptions of his novels resulted in indifferent television, adding, 'Quite honestly, Alex, I'm sure that my scripts are far, far better than yours (with all due respect to you as a novelist). And I'm equally sure you haven't read my scripts, even cursorily.' Every such rebuff was another wound in the side of the old lion. Now, past seventy years of age, Alexander still had an almost demonic need to write. This can be an awesome thing in a writer just setting out, who has the world in front of him to conquer. But Alexander had spent a lifetime making a living largely from historical novels or books about China and now seemed intent on driving himself further into the rut.

Alexander had high hopes of the BBC making a radio version of *Peerless Jim*. The boxer's story had a rival for the attention of BBC radio drama producer Adrian Mourby, and when the rival dropped out, the way was open for him. Early in June Mourby wrote a letter clearly explaining that the plot was too linear: Driscoll's smooth and uninterrupted ride to the top was followed by a gentle decline in such a predictable way that any dramatic interest was lost. He would, however, pass the script to his television colleagues. From this time on Alexander was to take a decreasing interest in television and film scripts and return to novels with a renewed emphasis. He had been told in so many words and from a couple of well-intentioned sources that a cobbler should stick to his last. Alexander was not in need of the relatively modest sum which television and radio performances might yield. With twenty or more books to his credit, some of which were still in print, the money from various options plus newspaper features and other little penny packets, the cash was still coming in.

As 1986 approached Alexander could easily have sat back, put the cover over his typewriter and not written another word. His agents, David Higham Associates and Curtis Brown (one hears more of the former and less of the latter after this date), were able stewards of his professional interests and his life-style was modest. Small successes, such as Radio 4's broadcasting of an adaptation of the Jim Driscoll story entitled 'Divine Intervention' for their *Morning Story* broadcast on 3 September 1985 did much to soothe wounded pride and maintain income. By the end of the year Alexander seems to have struck up a good relationship with the BBC, there having been some rocky patches in the past. As Christmas approached a letter from the producer of *Morning Story Wales* accepted a script entitled 'Eastern Promise'. Payment was only £84, not much even by 1985 prices, but as the year came to an end Alexander divined at least a few rays of hope. For one, there seemed to be a ready market for anything he could offer radio. As soon as television or film was mentioned, Alexander's reaction was to think in terms of massive productions, closely based on his own words as written in his novels. To match radio's more restrained charms he was able to devise plots that did not require a cast of thousands and by the very nature of the means of production did not require expensive sets, only sound effects.

Although he had been riding some rough weather with internationally known publishing houses, Alexander's stock was as high as ever at home, and 1986 began with the pleasant prospect of being published by a local house for consumption by a local readership. *Tales From Tiger Bay* was, as the name suggests, a series of short stories all with a Father O'Brien as the central character and set in a part of Cardiff which now only vestigially exists, the greatest part of it having been swallowed by the Cardiff Bay development. Chris Barber, who had previously successfully solicited Alexander's help for *Cordell Country*, published *Tales From Tiger Bay* under his Blorenge Books imprint. It was the high point of the relationship between the two.

For a couple of years amateur historian Richard Frame had been swimming in the same historical waters as Alexander, if for different reasons. Now, in 1987, the two met, the point of contact being the life of John Frost, the Chartist leader. Directly because of this meeting Alexander was to write *Requiem for a Patriot*, his twenty-fourth book. Frame had come to Newport as an art student and had been perplexed by the fact that nobody knew where the bones of the Newport-born Chartist leader lay. He reported:

> I and Derek Priest, a friend, found out that Frost moved to Bristol after returning from transportation in Van Diemen's Land (now Tasmania). We spent weeks scouring churchyards and cemeteries in and around Bristol. We found our answer where we should have looked in the first place. Frost's will, which is in Newport reference library, states exactly where he wished to be buried, at Horefield parish church near Stapleton. Frost's headstone itself was indecipherable, the only name I could make out being 'Henry Hunt'. We knew we had the right grave because Henry was Frost's son who had predeceased him and with whom Frost had willed that both he and his wife, Elizabeth, be buried. By a stroke of extreme good fortune the large flake of stone with Frost's name upon it was partly buried in the soil at the base of the stone. Two more winters and the headstone would have been completely unidentifiable. Newport Borough Council paid for a new gravestone which was carved by local stonemason Les Thomas. Neil Kinnock MP, the Labour Party leader who was fighting a general election that year, unveiled the headstone which had been draped with the Welsh flag.

At that time Newport History Society was talking about producing a souvenir publication leading up to the 150th anniversary of the Chartist Rising in 1989. Alexander had been contacted and asked to contribute a piece. One day, completely out of the blue, the phone rang and it was Alex calling from the Angel Hotel in Abergavenny. He was over from the Isle of Man promoting his latest book and pronounced himself eager to meet me. On a particularly nasty, rainy day outside the Newport Centre I met the man who was to become, with one other, the closest personal friend I ever had. I was immediately taken by his military bearing and the Englishness of the man. Somehow, I had imagined him to be of a darker, more Celtic appearance. We took to one another immediately. We were on the same wavelength, of course, about John Frost. I might have been slightly awed but he was chattering away happily. We visited various places in Newport connected with Frost and finally went to Thomas Street where he was born. Alex was eager for me to go to Bristol with him to see John Frost's grave. Of course, I said I would.

Newport Centre, where Frame and Alexander had met for the first time, was to house a production of *Rape of the Fair Country* later that same year. The production by the Chrysalis Theatre, with Ian Rowlands as Iestyn Mortymer and Roger Nott as Dada, performed to a full house. It was the first time the book had ever been converted into a play, although it was to be performed on stage several times over the ensuing decade with varying degrees of success.

In his foreword to the Chrysalis Theatre programme Alexander gave vent to his annoyance with television and film companies which he felt had let him down over the years.

For the past thirty years the film companies of Hollywood and Europe have bemoaned the cost of turning my book into a major film; eight librettos for its musical version have been written, with a horde of music and lyrics for stunning productions that never came about because, said the financiers, the cost was astronomical: television adaptations had been written, some actually bought, by networks and abandoned for one strange reason after another . . .

he fulminated before touching upon the possibility of undercover political censorship by 'the Mandarins of the Establishment' and concluding that this had 'quite probably been brought into play'. Nevertheless, the actor and producer Chris Morgan and his scriptwriter friend Philip Michel had achieved what had never been achieved before and Alexander was duly grateful to them.

The adaptation was a sell-out in Newport as it later was in Cardiff. Alexander's presence in south Wales coincided with publication of *This Proud and Savage Land,* published by Weidenfeld and Nicolson. The story, set in Wales, opens in 1804 with the marriage of Hywel Mortimer and Rhia Evans on a bright day in August, 'while the old Blorenge was putting away her summer clothes and decking herself in brown'.

Welsh hills were very much on Alexander's mind, although not the Welsh hills over which his literary imagination had ranged. Negotiations had been in hand for the purchase of a house at 1 Horseshoe Pass, Llangollen. On 30 July 1987 £38,815 – the net proceeds for the sale of the house at Ballabeg – were paid into Alexander's account and his plans for moving to north Wales seemed about to be realized. But the move to Llangollen never came about. Alexander's solicitor at the firm of Gwilym Hughes and Partners in Wrexham, Gethin Davies, who was to remain Alexander's solicitor and friend, pointed out that there had been some problem with the access road to the property. Alexander drew the necessary inferences and commenced negotiations for the purchase of the house at Railway Road, Wrexham, which was to be his and Donnie's last home. In the light of what was to happen exactly ten years later one's subconscious endows the names Llangollen and Horseshoe Pass with a dolefulness they do not in themselves deserve. It was at the top of the Horseshoe Pass on 9 July 1997 that Alexander was found dead.

In the ten years that were left to him Alexander was to see the death of his second wife, and was to continue to see his dreams of a television series or feature film of one or another of his books thwarted. There were to be compensations, though. As *This Proud and Savage Land* received a respectable sale, he slipped the first sheet of A4 paper into his battered old electric typewriter ready to hammer out his next book, *Requiem for a Patriot.* Six more books, including *Requiem* lay ahead of him. Whatever other misfortunes were to befall him, it was not fated that he should succumb to that which he feared most, that the ability to write might desert him.

In early October 1987 almost two hundred people crowded into the Cordell Country Inn, the pub on the Govilon to Blaenavon road which had been named in his honour. They were old friends in whose eyes he could do little wrong. The eyes that regarded the gathering from the head of the table as he rose to address them were those of a man advanced in years, who had seen much triumph and some tragedy. He had looked into these people's souls and had abstracted from them the unforgettable characters that raged and strutted, loved and suckled in his books, and he was pleased to be back among them from his self-imposed exile on the Isle of Man. They were his people, and he was their writer and the bond between them was indissoluble.

'Stickability' was a quality Alexander admired more than most (a raffish anarchism came top of the list). During his worst period in the mid to late 1980s when most literary people thought that he was on the ropes and might not come out fighting, he had believed in his own powers even though a large part of the general public apparently thought he had died. Precisely the stubbornness which had led him to believe that he could write television and film scripts better than those who were professionals now came to his aid. On 12 January 1988 his story, 'Caesar's Wife' went out as BBC Radio Wales *Morning Story*. The story is the very model of craftsmanship, something that should be shown to every aspirant to the short-story writer's art.

'The sun was like bottled glass, I remember, and the distant hills like hot loaves straight from the baker's dozen,' he wrote, and then moved into a virtuoso display of dialogue and characterization. If he was pleased with the broadcast, and with himself, he was entitled to be. *This Proud and Savage Land* had gone into its third edition, he was happy with Donnie in his new home, they spent much time together exploring the countryside around Wrexham, and he was eagerly anticipating the celebrations which would surround the 150th anniversary in 1989 of the Chartist Rising.

In a brief note to Herbert Williams, *Morning Story* producer at the BBC, he expressed himself 'on the crest of a wave! Next time we meet I will pay for the lunch!' As he embarked upon *Requiem for a Patriot*, published in 1988, Alexander had recovered much of his composure. He relished the task of hammering the story of John Frost into novel form. A chance discovery by Richard Frame in the National Library of Wales, Aberystwyth, of a letter which other researchers seemed to have disregarded brought a sense of immediacy to the work in progress.

Frame explained the importance of the document:

The signature at the bottom was that of 'Zephaniah Williams', one of the triumvirate who led the South Wales Chartists. It was a letter written to the ship's doctor of the *Mandarin*, the convict ship taking Frost, Williams and William Jones to exile in Van Diemen's Land. It was a startling admission in which Williams said the insurgents had intended to shoot magistrates and effectively proclaim a republic. It was shortly after discovering the letter that I met Alex. He told me he was thinking of doing a book about John Frost, and when I told him of what I had found at Aberystwyth he became very excited. He had already started his research but this gave it a big fillip – he felt he had a large historical chunk at which to bite. He regularly discussed the book and its progress particularly in the bits that had to do with Newport. He was methodical in the extreme. For instance, he wanted to know a lot about Stow Fair, which was held near the cathedral, just outside the town boundaries. I soon realized that a writer who wanted to know exactly where on Stow Hill, virtually to the yard, the fairs had been held was a stickler for detail. I had heard criticisms that Alexander Cordell sometimes bent historical facts to suit his dramatic purpose.

Frame, together with Dr David Osmond, a GP and local historian, became further embroiled in controversy surrounding the Chartists after Newport Local History Society, of which both were officers, suggested putting up a memorial to twenty Chartists who were buried in an unmarked grave in the cathedral precincts the night after the abortive rising.

On the night of 5 November 1839, when Newport was asleep, the soldiers slung the bodies of the dead Chartists into the mass grave. For many years afterwards people would put flowers on the grave despite it not being marked but gradually this habit died off and now nobody knows for sure where the men's bones lie. The intense local controversy about the Chartists, which divided into two camps – were they drunken rioters or revolutionaries? – is still a live issue after more than 150 years. The church gave us permission to put up a plaque near the lich-gate but insisted on having the final say as to its wording. We wanted words to the effect that the men were shot outside the Westgate and the diocesan authority wanted something much more non-committal. In the end we compromised, and agreed that the Chartists died in 'an exchange of shots'. While Alexander was not involved in all this toing and froing he made it quite clear that he favoured the history society's interpretation. The inscribed stone was unveiled in November 1988, actually the 149th anniversary, by Alexander and the mayor of Newport, Councillor Veronica Brydon.

All through that summer and autumn Alexander had been hard at work on his latest novel, which he had provisionally entitled *Moll Walbee* but which his publishers, Sphere, wanted to shorten simply to *Moll*. In a literal sense Alexander was returning to the Shrewsbury of his younger days in *Moll*, part of the action of which takes place in the

At the Chartists' resting place, with Councillor Veronica Brydon, Mayor of Newport, 1988.

man-made caves at Nesscliffe, ten miles north-west of the city. Alexander had been aware of these faintly sinister excavations and had motored out to them even before the war. Approached up steep steps carved from the sandstone, they made a deep impression on his subconscious. For many years their dramatic possibilities simmered away on some low flame at the back of his mind to reach boiling point with this story of Moll the adventuress, which combined Alexander's love of dramatic female characters with the picaresque. The military side of Alexander was tickled when with Donnie, Richard Frame and Mike Buckingham, he called at the Old Three Pigeons, the (inevitably)

145

On a 'recce' at the caves at Nesscliffe, during the writing of *Moll Walbee*.

haunted and ancient pub a few hundred yards from the caves. Alexander was so taken with the pub that he started his story there. A large part of the attraction, no doubt, was the cheerfully eccentric landlord who had purchased an army tank which had its gun pointed straight towards the caves.

Alexander threw himself into the writing of *Moll* with a will, his old zest restored, allowing himself to be carried along by the exploits of his mid-nineteenth-century heroine. His own doubts, and perhaps those of some of the people who considered his best years were past, were laid by the fact that Sphere offered an advance of £10,000, then not very far short of the national average annual wage. *Requiem for a Patriot*, Moll's immediate predecessor, had won an advance of only £5,000. Such a sudden inrush of funds was welcome because right at the end of 1988 Alexander crashed his Datsun car on a visit to his sister-in-law in Bournemouth. The most charitable description of Alexander's driving would be 'indifferent' and he had suffered bumps several times, especially as he got older. The Datsun was written off when Alexander reversed from a drive, across the road, and virtually demolished the gate and low wall on the far side of the road. The house owner's claim was settled amicably enough and Alexander began the New Year with a late-model buff-coloured Austin Montego which he promptly christened the Cement Mixer.

On the exact anniversary of the Chartist Rising Alexander walked down Stow Hill, the route that had been followed by the insurrectionaries in 1839, in the company of Neil Kinnock MP, leader of the Labour Party, Mrs Glenys Kinnock, Paul Flynn, MP for Newport West, and representatives of what were then Blaenau Gwent, Torfaen, Islwyn and Newport Councils. The affair was an emotional one, the procession being led by a group of schoolchildren in Victorian dress. As he walked in the company of Councillor Rosemary Butler, Newport's mayor, Alexander was beaming proudly, fully convinced of the fact that it was largely due to his literary efforts that the Chartists were being remembered at all.

With his books going well and public adulation at a new high Alexander at first paid little attention to a nasty little situation brewing as the 1980s came to a close. It was soon, however, to obsess him. A letter from the Penguin Group from Mr Trevor Glover, UK group managing director, informed Alexander personally that Penguin Group was in negotiations with Maxwell Communications Corporation which was considering buying the venerable paperback firm. The move horrified Alexander, who detested Maxwell and regarded him as traitor to the Labour cause. Indeed it was of some satisfaction to Alexander that he outlived Maxwell.

As he slipped the first pages of what was to become *Beloved Exile* into his typewriter Alexander knew that he was on a roll, and it was with a feeling of renewed confidence that he started the work. In January 1990 Barbara Boote of Sphere wrote to Alexander that she understood the novel in hand was going well. In August the book had not only been written and revised but was in her hands. 'I've just finished *Beloved Exile* and I think it's great, both in terms of your writing and the contrasts of the brutality, hatred, fighting, frostbiting snow and Iestyn's love for Mari and Durrani and the triumph over all odds,' she wrote, giving both an attestation of Alexander's skill and a reasonable résumé of the book. It was, in fact, the first time Iestyn Mortymer had appeared in a novel since *Rape of the Fair Country* over thirty years before. At the end of the book it is Iestyn who becomes Alexander's *alter ego* and sits down to write *Rape of the Fair Country*. It is almost as though the author was apologizing to Iestyn for neglecting him for so long by endowing him with a literary talent.

The encouraging words from Barbara Boote were the last Alexander was to have from this quarter for some time. At the time of the implosion of Maxwell's empire Barbara Boote had written that she did not know what would happen to Sphere, a part of Macdonald, which was a member of Maxwell Macmillan Corporation PLC. 'But my strong feeling is that we shall be sold off in one publishing group to someone. There are a lot of possible contenders, mostly good ones, so odds are that I will remain in place and that your books are perfectly safe . . .'

The dice, however, were being shaken by mightier gods than Alexander or perhaps even Barbara Boote suspected. Maxwell's collapse had caused an earthquake but there was another epicentre, the shock waves from which were to disturb the writer's calm and challenge his new-found sense of security. Publishing houses were now merging, going bankrupt, starting up, buying up and selling at a truly bewildering rate. What had once been a stable industry for the employment of gentlemen and young ladies was now becoming as ruthless and hard-edged as the rest of British industry. When both these seismic events activated at the same time, Alexander's house began to shake. *Beloved Exile* was at a late stage of preparation in April 1992 when it was held up by Little, Brown, the new owners of Macdonald following Maxwell's death.

Alexander's disquiet at the new letterheading on the correspondence from Barbara Boote increased to alarm when he read the contents. It was dated 8 April 1992 and began, 'I'm afraid this is a perfectly horrible letter to be writing'. It went on to say that Little, Brown had bought the bulk of Macdonald's publishing business and there were a few books that would not fit into the 'new environment' and those included many of Alexander's works. 'Specifically, this boils down to our not publishing *Dreams of Fair Women*, *Beloved Exile*, *Race of the Tiger*, *Sinews of Love*, *The Bright Cantonese*, *The Dream and the Destiny*, *Rogue's March* or *To Slay the Dreamer*.' Barbara Boote's letter contained even worse news, which was that Macdonald would not be paying out any outstanding money on the books and Alexander would have to join the enormous queue of those with claims on the Maxwell estate. 'It is horrifying how many people have been so affected by Maxwell's crumbling empire . . . I do wish you every success,' she concluded, with the 'do' underlined. The letter was a parting of the ways for editor and writer who had shared a professional yet warm relationship. Only one more letter was to pass between them when, a few months later, some books which had been at the publishing house but which were Alexander's personal property were returned. *Beloved Exile* was eventually published by Piatkus after Alexander decided the best thing to do about Maxwell was to buy his own rights back and look for a new publisher. Alexander grumbled about Piatkus's small advance but was relieved to see the book in print. 'At least there is publishing after Maxwell,' he said in a telephone conversation with

Mike Buckingham. Alexander sometimes swallowed his pride and accepted small advances if it meant being published. A shortage of funds could mean famine of a kind, but not being published to such a prolific and dedicated writer was a form of death.

One little incident which cropped up while *Beloved Exile* was in galley proof caused Alexander to fire off a rapid and indignant letter to Judy Piatkus. At some point during the book's production a printer or an editor had placed a more vulgar expression where Alexander had intended 'bloody'. The fact that Victorian troopers swore then much as it can be assumed troopers swear now was beside the point. 'I have little doubt that the speaker would have used the word somebody inserted but I did not do so in the script and wish to ensure it does not appear in the published work,' he huffed. 'Nobody can accuse me of being prim but in three million published words I have never used such a word.' In fact, and as Alexander acknowledged, Piatkus was not to blame. The word had been typeset at Sphere before the manuscript passed into Piatkus's hands. Suspicion has to rest on a demoralized printer or editor faced with the sack in the wake of Maxwell's death. *Beloved Exile*, when it was eventually published, was trailed as 'the magnificent sequel to *Rape of the Fair Country*' and had as its mainspring a bitter hatred for Queen Victoria which with Alexander was an almost personal matter. *Send Her Victorious*, his final book, which deals with a French-inspired plot to put Queen Victoria on trial for her life, further indulges this antipathy and was his parting shot.

Any disappointment he might have felt at the small rewards which were to flow from *Beloved Exile* were compensated for by the fact that his next book, *Dreams of Fair Women*, another book set in Hong Kong, was on the stocks. Alexander was always able to put disappointment to one side once a new book was under way. Each book, as the final words 'The End' were typed and it was parcelled and sent off to his publisher, was going to be the best, the one to 'knock their socks off' even if he later admitted it had been nothing more than a pot-boiler. It was a belief fuelled by a fierce determination that was to keep him going through the most despairing of times. Actually, given the fact that his eightieth birthday was approaching, affairs were far from desperate on the professional front.

Even Alexander had accepted that retirement must come in some form and he had been negotiating for a flat in Bournemouth. The rationale for this was an assumption that he would die before Donnie, who would at least have the comfort of being near her sister. As always, Alexander hoped that a film or a television series might be made of his work, although by this time a certain degree of resignation had crept in. On this matter he was cheered by a letter from John Barnes in America who in March 1992 wrote Alexander a long letter suggesting in effect that he and Alexander pool their rights in *Rape of the Fair Country* and split any proceeds down the middle. At this stage Alexander still had reason to believe that Alan Jones, a Newport man who had played saxophone with the 1960s hit band Amen Corner, and who was the latest aspirant, might make a film. 'If we make it I'll buy you a fish and chip dinner in some Soho joint and we'll drink bad wine together,' Alexander told Barnes.

Alexander's local stock was riding high. A musical adaptation of *Rape of the Fair Country*, written by Rob and Rozi Morris and performed by the drama club of Gwent College of Higher Education at its Caerleon campus, played to a packed house with Alexander in the front row, receiving the audience's adulation. Also at this time Alexander had been invited by Roger Cucksey, Keeper of Art at Newport's Art Gallery, to provide a foreword to a museum publication about the local artist John Flewitt Mullock. Alexander responded with enthusiasm, especially when told that Mullock was living and working in Newport at the time of the Chartist Rising and may actually have been an eye-witness from a window above the corner of Skinner Street from which viewpoint he sketched events.

Buoyed up by respectable sales of *Beloved Exile* and unfazed by the fact that 582 copies of *Moll* had remained unsold and had been offered back to him at 10 per cent of the published price of £13, Alexander threw himself into a new project with an Australian background. In the same way as a brief visit to Spain had provided sufficient inspiration for *To Slay the Dreamer*, a lightning visit to Australia had stoked his imagination with images of a pitiless climate, primeval flora and fauna, cruelly mistreated aboriginals and red-necked, beer-swilling, brutal white settlers. For Alexander, white adventurers and colonists could be brave, resourceful and intelligent and perhaps even spasmodically compassionate, but they were rarely right in any moral sense. In a letter to David O'Leary, whom he had engaged as his agent and who remained in that role right up until the time of Alexander's death, he remarked on the inevitability of a writer being left-wing. With the same sense of almost Marxian determinism (although he was certainly no Marxist) he was equally certain that whites were to blame for every evil countenanced during Australia's history. This regrettable Aryan failing was to be partially atoned for in his new book to be called 'Sun Chariot'.

'Make no mistake, the book would be an indictment of white domination in the homeland of the Australian aborigines; the profound and outrageous cruelties practised against an uncivilized and unprotected people in the name of greed', he wrote. By the end of 1992 he had written six chapters. The central character was to be Rick or Richard, a half-breed whose father is killed by the aboriginals for his adultery. Rick is initiated into the tribe by circumcision but by various twists of the plot reverts to white society. Unfortunately for Rick, he 'goes walkabout' every time there is a full moon. This might well have led to some interesting possibilities had the book been completed. For this expiatory work Alexander was quite prepared to 'go native'. In a relatively rare example of unconscious humour Alexander wrote to O'Leary: 'To go native is a terrific challenge, and it will be said the task is beyond me; it is not. Despite all criticism, I put myself into the skin of a Welshman successfully.' The idea of the brisk former officer with the clipped moustache and impeccably British bearing slipping into the skin of an aborigine raises a smile. The project died a death which is probably just as well for Alexander's reputation. By April 1993 it is evident from an interview with Mario Basini, the *Western Mail* feature writer, that 'Sun Chariot' had been relegated to the Dreamtime. Basini, presumably quoting Alexander, refers merely to 'thoughts' about writing an Australian novel and his article was the last time the project was ever mentioned in print, although as a subject it continued to occupy the author's mind for a few months more.

Chapter Fifteen

As the mid-1990s approached it became apparent that the raped and pillaged land which Alexander had used as the backdrop to his novels might have one more treasure to yield. Tourism in north Gwent had a very slow start and for many years the only real attraction was the Big Pit Mining Museum, formerly a working pit, just outside Blaenavon. By the middle of the decade, however, the nearby Blaenavon Ironworks was in the middle of a process of restoration and both Torfaen and Blaenau Gwent Councils were pondering how they might capitalize on their industrial past. Alexander threw himself into various projects to increase the tourist profile of the area with gusto: 'If Catherine Cookson can have a country named after her, I can have a Cordell Country,' he declared. The streak of vanity which affected Alexander no more than most who achieve a certain celebrity in life was generally concealed, but given full play in a variety of projects on paper which included a complete reconstruction of the Drum and Monkey public house which had once stood outside the main entrance to Blaenavon Ironworks, Chartist caves with wax figures forging weapons for the assault upon Newport, dioramas and displays and most of all, large signs saying 'Welcome to Cordell Country'. In a letter to Phil Clark, director of the Sherman Theatre, Alexander was effusive about the plans for publicizing north Gwent as a tourist destination, much of which would feature him and his work, but he was even more excited about another project. The twin 'iron towns' of Blaenavon and Nantyglo could be inseparably linked in the public's mind by means of a musical to be presented in Swansea as part of the celebrations for the 1995 Year of Literature. 'It strikes me that the linking of your project with that of tourism should be the main thought to advancement as a whole, since one automatically serves the other . . . How could the tourist strategy be better enhanced than through the medium of a musical of the book representing both towns?', he told Phil Clark rhetorically. In a BBC Wales broadcast in 1995 in which both Alexander and Phil Clark spoke of their plans for a musical of *Rape of the Fair Country,* Alexander remarked that there was nobody he would rather have interpret his work than Clark. John Barnes, with whom the date to eat a fish and chip dinner and drink bad wine in Soho had not yet been kept and who by now owned half the film and television rights to *Rape of the Fair Country* had a vested interest in the musical and was part of the negotiations. As had been so often the case before, the project failed through lack of funds. Alexander was disappointed but always spoke well of Clark and continued to hope the two might work together. The producer later sent Alexander a little water-colour, a windblown and twisted thorn in the middle ground with a barbed-wire fence, an archetypal Welsh rural scene. The more observant who have seen the painting since his death have remarked how similar the scene is to the one from which, five years later, Alexander's body was recovered. Alexander particularly liked the little picture and would draw visitors' attention to it.

As the author's eightieth birthday loomed, his mood was bullish. *Beloved Exile* had achieved a reasonable sale as had *Dreams of Fair Women;* another book which would see the light of day as *The Love That God Forgot,* set partially on the island of Flatholm in the Bristol Channel, was fermenting in his mind. With all the indicators set fair, Alexander was living with an almost boyish glee, avid for long expeditions into the countryside when Frame and Buckingham came to visit from south Wales (something that happened every six weeks or so) and even investigating the mysteries of new technology. In Australia, while researching the doomed 'Sun Chariot', Alexander had called in a small outback library and asked for some local information. The assistant replied that what he needed was not to hand but could be faxed from Adelaide. Alexander watched transfixed as the message was faxed off and the reply came back. After mulling the matter over a lunchtime drink a month later in Wrexham, Alexander announced to Frame and Buckingham that he had decided to buy a fax machine and the trio piled into Alexander's Austin Montego and headed for Chester while Donnie was left behind in the bungalow to prepare the evening meal. Frame recalls:

Alexander was still toying with the idea of the Australian book and I pointed out that he could save money and time by faxing for the information he needed. What I hadn't bargained for in my enthusiasm is that we were all technologically inept, I slightly less so than Alexander and Mike. In a glow of enthusiasm Alexander bought a top-of-the-range model which looked simple and straightforward in the store but which was a nightmare of wires and connections once we got it back to Wrexham and out of the box. I spent hours with a screwdriver swearing and scratching my head while the other two laughed and drank whisky.

Drives out into the country were invariably jolly affairs with Alexander and his friends describing themselves as being on a 'recce'.

Hong Kong, 1990s. Alexander's and Donnie's last visit.

Serious work was often done but a visit to a pub was an indispensable part of the proceedings. During these reconnaissance missions Alexander usually drank whisky-and-ginger. As the evening wore on the talk would turn to books and Alexander would try out possible plot lines on Frame and Buckingham. It was after the two had departed for south Wales and Alexander was left alone except for Donnie that an anxiety began to form. For a man of eighty his own health was reasonably good, although he had been prescribed tablets for a persistent heart condition. His concerns were not for his own health but for that of Donnie, who late in 1993 had cataracts removed from her eyes.

The condition was not, of course, life-threatening, but Alexander's understanding of medical matters was rudimentary to say the least. 'Alexander was a man who was ruled by the heart. Anatomically he could barely grasp the fact that the heart was a kind of pump which drives blood around the body,' Frame was later to say. Anticipating a decline in Donnie's health, Alexander put the The Conifers on the market at the end of 1993 with an asking price of £97,000 freehold. The estate agent's blurb described the bungalow as being owned by 'one of North Wales' most famous authors', and requiring a personal inspection in order for the prospective buyer to appreciate it. The plan was to remove to Bournemouth so that Donnie could be near her sister when, as Alexander thought inevitable, he died first. Frame and Buckingham had reservations about the scheme, knowing full well that Alexander would greatly miss Wales. 'I'm not wild about Bournemouth either, but I have to think of Donnie,' he confided.

Frame in particular was able to help Alexander in the early stages of *The Love that God Forgot*, his twenty-seventh book, which opens on Flatholm and proceeds through a plot which touches upon the subject of incest before ending happily ever after on the island where it began. Frame had been a member of the Flatholm Society and had spent a lot of time on the island helping with the renovation of the old farmhouse. He remembers:

In April 1995 Alexander and I caught the boat across to Flatholm. It was a day of low, scudding clouds and I think he was enjoying the romance of it. You could see he was already plotting out the book. Suddenly he asked me if he could speak to the pilot, which I quickly arranged. Alexander asked the man where was the deepest water off the island where a ship might be sunk. A few months later when the book came out Alexander had sunk a boat right where the pilot said it should be. Once on the island Alexander decided that where an old foghorn station still stands was the ideal location for the Mortymer cottage. Alexander was entranced by the island and its romantic possibilities, the blustery weather serving only to heighten his enthusiasm. He'd just mentally marked out his ground when a guide who knew him pointed him out to a group of tourists. The minute we got back to the farmhouse Alexander was surrounded by a crowd of autograph hunters and loving every minute of it it.

The Love that God Forgot, when it appeared in 1995, was supposed to round off the neatly chronological story of the Mortymers. In fact,

Alexander wrote *The Love that God Forgot* before *Land of Heart's Desire*. Given the fact that *This Proud and Savage Land* predated *Rape of the Fair Country* in terms of fictional chronology but was actually written twenty-eight years later some confusion on the part of the book-buying public was understandable.

By the end of 1994 Alexander began to worry more about his own health. Old age was at last catching up with him. In a letter to Edwin Buckhalter, chairman of Severn House Publishing, his last publisher, he cried off what would have been a fairly exhausting round of interviews and book signings. 'I have decided not to undertake book signings. I have taken on a big task of two novels in so short a time. I can handle any amount of radio interviews, but my doctor advised me to cut them [television interviews and signings] out,' he wrote to Buckhalter. Right at the end of 1994 Alexander had been on the point of buying a flat at Milford-on-Sea in Hampshire, to be near Donnie's sister, but by the spring of the following year had cooled on the idea even though the Wrexham bungalow remained on the market. After rejecting the Hampshire option he opened negotiations to buy a flat at 129 Haymoor Road, Oakdale, Poole, but this scheme, too, fell by the wayside when Donnie was taken into Maelor Hospital, Wrexham, having been complaining of abdominal pain for some time. Tests revealed a situation very much more serious than either of them could have thought. Almost immediately cancer was diagnosed. As she lay in Luke Ward, visibly shrunken, Alexander virtually camped by his wife's bed. His sense of helplessness as Donnie became more ill was added to by the confusion which her absence caused. Their days together had run to a well-established pattern. Ordinarily they would each rise before 7.30 a.m. and share a light breakfast before showering and Alexander going to his work room where a single bed had been installed and where he usually slept. He would attack whichever novel was under his hand for three hours at least before dealing with correspondence, which was often considerable. For a man who insisted on even the most casual meal at home being served with a modicum of formality Alexander was surprisingly addicted to American-style diners and often lunched at a Little Chef or Happy Eater. Lunch was followed by a drive and perhaps some shopping before returning home to sandwiches and television. Now, with Donnie desperately ill, the routine fell apart utterly. Although a woman had for years been employed to do the housework and a gardener to keep the borders and lawns at the rear and front of the house tidy, Donnie kept financial records and also ensured that Alexander kept to his regime of pills. With her in hospital, Alexander was taking his prescribed pills in any order and frequently not at all. Frame, who with Buckingham had travelled from Gwent to Wrexham at Alexander's request very shortly after Donnie had been taken into hospital, made it his business to order the pills and try to ensure that Alexander ate a balanced diet.

In the evenings the trio invariably dined at the Sleepy Panda Chinese restaurant in Wrexham but although Alexander could be cheered up for short periods his underlying pain was obvious. On 21 October at around eight o'clock the three went to Maelor Hospital where Donnie had been moved into a side ward. Frame, a trained nurse, had worked with geriatrics, and to his experienced eye the end was already very near. Alexander sat by her bed, patting her hand, his eyes misted with tears. As they left, Donnie raised a hand and managed a smile. Just as they arrived in Newport at midnight, Donnie died. She was eighty years of age and had been Alexander's wife for a quarter of a century. A distraught Alexander telephoned Frame a few hours after the death, his voice shaking with sorrow but also anger. When it became obvious that Donnie had very little time left, the hospital had called Alexander who drove to the Maelor but was unable to gain entrance. He had not been with Donnie at the moment of her death.

Balance usually implies harmony but the equilibrium which existed in the months after Donnie's death was a strange and portentous one, like the still, heavy weather that precedes the breaking of a storm. On one side, Alexander's own health was breaking up at an alarming rate. Irregular patterns of self-medication often combined with alcohol were causing alarming delusions. Quite suddenly Alexander seemed what he had never seemed to be before – a very old man. More poignant therefore was the fact that as 1996 passed his literary flame burned brighter than for some time. Not only that but the achievements of the past were being recognized at an accelerating rate. The mortal Cordell was becoming weaker but the immortal one was emerging from its chrysalis. Two days after Donnie's death Alexander himself was admitted to Maelor Hospital suffering from hypertension. Within two days he had signed himself out with a remark that showed that, despite his tragic circumstances, he had not lost his sense of humour, that 'he couldn't stand the sight of any more old people'.

Within days of his discharge against medical advice, Frame and Buckingham travelled north and found Alexander well composed. Donnie's ashes were in a plastic container, surrounded by flowers on a table in the dining room. Once more Frame was worried about the pills that Alexander was taking in the wrong order and the fact that some of

157

the things in his refrigerator were lethally past their 'sell-by' dates. The two visitors cleared the fridge and bought a stack of TV suppers and, unsuccessfully as it turned out, instructed Alexander in the use of his own microwave cooker. More alarmingly, Frame and Buckingham learned that Alexander had fallen over several times and on one occasion had hit his head on the lounge door, breaking the plywood. 'At one point he had clearly suffered a stroke. He told me that he thought he would die on the floor with nobody to help,' Frame recalls.

The degree to which Alexander's health was failing made his professional recovery at this time even more remarkable. It was as though, sensing that death was near, he somehow donned a mantle of superhuman invincibility. Within three months of Donnie's death and his own hospitalization, he had submitted a synopsis for a novel to be called 'A Petticoat Rebellion', based on the history of the suffragettes, to Severn House Publishers. Although the option had run out on the Sherman production of *Rape of the Fair Country,* he was also busy negotiating with Terry Underwood of Newport for an amateur musical production based on the book. (It was in fact staged posthumously.) On the literary front, Monique Girault, who had been a friend for almost thirty years and had been in touch with Alexander regularly for several months, sowed the germ of a literary idea which flourished in Alexander's mind. All his life he had entertained a loathing for Queen Victora and enthusiastically threw himself into plotting a novel which debunked the Victorian myth. The title *Send Her Victorious* was suggested by Buckingham but the detailed research using French sources was wholly carried out Monique Girault. 'The Petticoat Rebellion' was put to one side while Alexander charged into the writing of *Send Her Victorious.* It was an exhausting task undertaken with the most intense professional commitment and when it was finished he lapsed into depression.

One evening he rang Frame drunk and tearful. In response to the call Frame rushed northwards and found Alexander in low spirits. The customary meal at the Sleepy Panda enlivened him somewhat and by the end of the meal the two were chatting about the possibility of another book on a historical theme. The next day Frame drove Alexander to Harlech where Alexander talked about his convalescent period during the war. In the mundane surroundings of a fish and chip shop but with Snowdon a cloud-crowned presence in the far distance, Frame tried to get Alexander interested in a book about Owain Glyndŵr. Walking back to the car, Alexander slowed down and had to sit on a wall to recover his breath while Frame fetched the car. 'I had

With Richard Frame, Lavernock Point, 6 April 1996.

never thought of him as an old man. Now I realized he was not only that but also a very sick old man,' Frame said. And yet the old man, exhausted and heartbroken, was still, on St David's Day 1997, able to stand and receive the applause of the Welsh public as, at the Swansea Grand Theatre, a joint production by the Grand Theatre and West Glamorgan Theatre of *Rape of the Fair Country* was cheered to the echo. As the cast bowed for the third curtain call, Helen Griffin, who played the part of Mrs Mortymer, flung up her hands and hushed the applause. 'Before you applaud us, there is somebody else here who deserves greater applause than us,' she said. 'The author – Alexander Cordell', and with that she pointed to the circle where Alexander rose. The silence, as he stood slightly awkwardly to attention, was palpable. And then a storm was unleashed. Cheers rang round the auditorium with clapping like waves breaking, as indeed they were breaking on the far shore of his mortal life. It seemed already that he was with the gods. Some people cried. As Alexander was swept from the theatre he was introduced to the singer and songwriter Martin Joseph who had written a song about Dic Penderyn which he had been inspired to write after reading *The Fire People*. Alexander, who had heard the song and truly admired it, smiled and said, 'I love your work'. It was Joseph who sang, one blazingly hot day a few weeks after Alexander's death, on the site of Penderyn's scaffold in St Mary's Street, Cardiff. The ghost of Cordell was at that little gathering, called to mark the anniversary of the execution of the Welsh martyr.

With Mike Buckingham at Lavernock Point, 1996.

Welsh matters were very much on the author's mind after his wife's death despite the physical and emotional pain. In a letter to Dafydd Wigley, leader of Plaid Cymru, he wrote: 'I come straight from my armchair to the typewriter to tell you how much I admired the essential sincerity of your wonderful party speech' (which he had seen on television). Shortly after that Alexander joined Plaid Cymru, the only political party of which he was ever a member. 'If the Welsh will have me I would like to become a member of Plaid,' he said, with no false humility, in the letter to Wigley.

The date 15 June 1997 will always be referred to by Frame and Buckingham as Rainbow Day, one endowed with an almost transcendental quality. During the final weekend ghosts drawn from Welsh history walked the timeless landscape of Snowdonia as Alexander was conveyed in Buckingham's Volvo with Frame joking in the back and keeping up a constant discourse about Owain Glyndŵr, to the home of radio journalist Ian Skidmore on Anglesey. Skidmore had written a popular history of Glyndŵr and had some source material which he had promised to lend Alexander. Skidmore and Alexander had met only once before but the two took to each other instantly. The visit was convivial, with Skidmore's wife, Celia, taking pictures of the four men. It had been a rainy, blowy day and, once over the Menai Bridge on the way home, Frame suggested stopping at every pub between Bangor and

Wrexham which had the word 'Head' in its name. After Betws-y-coed no public house bearing the required word had appeared and the suggestion was passed back and forth that perhaps another name should be selected. At that moment a rainbow appeared and Buckingham remarked: 'I hope there's a pot of gold in the form of a pub at the end of that.' There was. The Turk's Head, on the road to Corwen, never had more gleeful visitors. So good an omen did the three consider the rainbow that Frame thought the gods might be in a generous mood and risked £1 in the one-armed-bandit. The expected pot of gold (or cupro-nickel anyway) did not transpire. Ambrosia in the form of pints of beer, however, did. The following day the trio drove to Sycharth, to the south-west of Oswestry, which had been Owain Glyndŵr's home and to the church at Llansilin where the leader had worshipped. Again on the trail of Owain Glyndŵr they visited Kentchurch between Abergavenny and Hereford which is thought by some to be the last resting-place of Glyndŵr and later the same day the Templar church at nearby Garway. The air was still and suddenly it became cold and dark. As they stood in the dim chapel a thunderclap rent the silence. They looked at one another. It was as though an omen had been delivered, some sort of a warning or intimation of loss. At the end of that weekend Alexander drove back to Wrexham but remained in almost daily contact with Frame and Buckingham, enthusing about the Owain Glyndŵr project. At the end of the first week in July a seemingly revived Alexander slipped a piece of paper into his old electric typewriter and dashed off a note to David O'Leary, his agent, with a copy to John Barnes. It was a brisk and businesslike note. Two days later, Alexander Cordell was found dead.

Postcript

A low, golden winter light suffused Wrexham and the hills beyond on Thursday 13 November, the day of the inquest into the death of George Alexander Graber. The Law Courts at Wrexham are bare and sterile, wreathed in misery and human failure. Alexander's inquest was scheduled for 10 a.m. and was the first to be heard, although when Mr John Bevan Hughes, the coroner for North Central Wales, entered and bowed to the few people in the public seats and to the scattering of pressmen, it was almost half-past. The first piece of evidence to be read out was a statement from Georgina, Alexander's only daughter, who gave her father's date and place of birth and added that he had left home to join the Army as quickly as possible to escape an unhappy childhood. He had served twice in the Army and after the war had been a quantity surveyor in Shrewsbury, Abergavenny and Hong Kong. On 7 March 1937 her father had married her mother, Rosina Gladys Wells, born in 1907. After Rosina's death her father had married Donnie. By this time her father was an established author and they had lived at Bangor, the Isle of Man and lastly The Conifers in Railway Road, Rhosddu, Wrexham. She had last spoken to her father on 2 July one week before his body was recovered, and found him in good spirits although she knew he had a heart condition.

The next statement to be read was from Monique Girault who said she had been introduced to Alexander's work while a teacher at Chepstow in the 1960s; she had shortly afterwards met the author and they quickly became friends. In the early 1970s he had retired to a caravan in the Forest of Dean and she had lost touch with him, but the contact had been re-established quite recently when she had brought a party of French schoolchildren to Gwent at a time when Alexander was inaugurating the Cordell Country Trail. Since then she had telephoned often and been to stay with him at Wrexham. She had last spoken to him on 1 or 2 July and had made arrangements to stay. When she had last seen him he had been fit although prone to breathlessness. On 12 July neighbours called her and told her of Alexander's death. 'I cannot believe he killed himself. To my knowledge I have never known him happier. He was looking forward to our visit. Things were working out well for him', she wrote. Madame Girault said she had come to Britain on 10 August and, together with Police Constable Ann O'Mahoney from Llangollen police station had gone to the spot where the body had been found. The climb over a gate and along the back of a stream and then across a stream would have been painful and difficult, especially since Alexander had been carrying a bag. She also doubted that Alexander, who was elderly and frail and could even be described as clumsy, would have been able to undo the tightly knotted rope which had secured the gate through, or over, which he would have to make his way. In the preceding months Madame Girault had become perturbed about the circumstances of the death, and was particularly suspicious of the secret service which, she felt, may never have forgiven Alexander for the anti-establishment stand he had taken in *Rape of the Fair Country* and subsequent works. Mr Hughes, the coroner, read the statement dispassionately and afterwards made no comment.

John Cyril Roberts, who farms land above the Horseshoe Pass said that on 9 July he and his brother Frank had been repairing fences near the quarry spoil tip and had spotted what they at first thought was a bale of hay in a green plastic wrapper fallen in the rivulet going down the hillside. They had gone across to find the body of an elderly man in a curious position. 'He was on his knees with his head on the floor of the ditch and kneeling like a Muslim on a prayer-mat. I didn't notice his face. There was a bottle beside him and a haversack on the wall and some photographs propped up against the bottle. We left the scene without touching the body and called the police.'

John Hughes, a neighbour, was a friend of Alexander's to whom he often had reason to be grateful. The ex-miner held a spare set of keys to The Conifers and would keep an eye on the premises if Alexander was away. (Alexander was serious about security and had fitted his house with an alarm. Even so, he had retained the 1-2-3-4 four-figure code sequence the manufacturer had supplied – hardly an uncrackable code.) Mr Hughes said Alexander would sometimes get depressed,

perhaps once a month, but he got over it very quickly. On July 2 Alexander telephoned my wife and asked her to ask me to go round to his house because he was feeling depressed. At about 6 p.m. I went round and had a drink with him. He had a drink of whisky but might not have touched it. He said he had been 'let down' but was not more specific. He kept looking at the pictures of his two wives which were on the wall.

On 10 July, a day after the body had been discovered, he was contacted by the Coroner's officer who asked him how the body might be identified and Mr Hughes told him about the war wound which had then been used to identify Alexander's body. Later, when asked to open the house by the police, he had done so and found a note which had been accompanied by pictures of Rosina and Donnie. 'Often he would say he'd had enough,' Mr Hughes told the inquest. 'He'd have a grumble but he would always pick himself up again. There was nothing about this particular occasion which caused me any extra concern.'

Police Constable Ann O'Mahoney, who in August had escorted Monique Girault and her husband, Claude, to the place of Alexander's death, gave her evidence in the clear, precise manner of a trained police officer. At 17.40 hours on 9 July she had gone to a place a quarter of a mile off the A452 following a report that a body had been found. She spoke to some ambulancemen and made her way to where a gate had been secured by a rope. Replying to the point raised by Madame Girault, PC O'Mahoney thought the rope which had secured the gate would not have been especially difficult to undo, although she chose to climb it. 'Mr Graber was on his knees with his head resting on the bed of the ditch in which there was one or two inches of water. The body was in an obvious resting-place below a tree. There was a shopping bag nearby, a half-consumed bottle of Napoleon brandy and two photographs.'

A bottle of Temazepam sleeping tablets with seven tablets remaining was recovered from the body. With the exception of the statement by Madame Girault which evidently, in the view of the coroner, pointed to a most unlikely manner of death, the whole tenor of the inquest up until that point appeared to lead to only one conclusion, which was that George Alexander Graber had taken his own life, possibly while the balance of his mind had been disturbed. But then, just like the dénouement of a novel, worthy of the master of words himself, a new and surprising set of facts began to emerge, which would lead to what, the coroner was later to admit, had been one of the strangest inquests at which he had ever officiated. Unfolding medical evidence, first from a general practitioner who testified that Alexander had never suffered any psychological illness nor had received any treatment for depression, began to point towards a natural death. Dr Anthony Howell Burdge, the pathologist, said he had commenced his post-mortem examination the day after the body had been recovered. Rigor mortis had disappeared and there were early signs of decomposition. No marks were found which might suggest violence. An examination of the lungs showed some congestion, but nothing to indicate drowning. And then, in a completely matter-of-fact voice, Dr Burdge destroyed the picture which had formed in most people's minds, which was that Alexander had committed suicide. 'A toxicology report showed that no alcohol was present and no drugs apart from a very small trace consistent with Mr Graber having taken one sleeping tablet. We can exclude death being due to the presence of drugs and alcohol. Despite the circumstances, tests for these were negative.'

Collectively, those in that forlorn room made a quiet intake of breath. In the minds of some the question must have occurred: could Madame Girault, who suspected that Alexander Cordell the radical author had been done away with by the agents of the vengeful state be, after all, correct? Dr Burdge adjusted his glasses and continued. What had been found was a degree of heart enlargement so great, and disease so advanced, that death could have happened at any time. 'I therefore believe that death was due to natural causes.' Dr Burdge agreed to a suggestion by the coroner that Alexander's heart could have given out with the exertion of climbing the fence. Mr Hughes had been a warm and comforting coroner, putting witnesses at their ease and obviously fully aware of the eminence of the subject of his inquiry.

By this time the atmosphere in the court room had changed. No longer merely witnesses, the people sitting there were members of an audience, gradually being enveloped in a story. In his lifetime Alexander would often say, 'Tell me a story that will bring old men from the fire and children from their play', and this surely, was such a story. Mr Hughes, although maintaining the dignity and impartiality befitting a coroner, was clearly as captured by the twist in the tail of this story as were the spectators and witnesses when he said, having restated the place and date of the death and the formal finding of death through natural causes:

> This has been a curious inquest in that the actions of Mr Graber seem to point in a particular direction. He had left his car, taking some brandy and sleeping tablets with him and some photographs, and went to a location that must have taken him a great deal of effort to reach. A note had been left at his house which could be taken as interpreting that he intended to take his own life. He had put two family photographs where he could see them but I believe that at that point nature intervened and he died quite naturally. I find therefore that George Alexander Graber died as a result of natural causes. It is ironic that a man who was such a story-teller should have such a story told about his own life right at the very end.

Afterwards the authors of this book were interviewed by the BBC and HTV and by the *Daily Telegraph* and thus were delayed in driving

Alexander Cordell, 1914–1997.
Relaxing over the supper table at Wrexham, 1992.

to the place where Alexander had died. It had been an almost inevitable part of any visit to Alexander that on the Saturday, having arrived on the Friday night, Frame and Buckingham would drive with him over the Horseshoe Pass and into Llangollen. When approaching the Ponderosa, a restaurant at the top of the Horseshoe Pass, Alexander would often want to stop and admire the rolling beauty of the hills, at the time of his death clothed with the rich green mantle of summer, but perhaps at their best when the russet of the dead bracken is fired by autumn light which also glances off the dying leaves on the trees in the valley below in a glory of reds and golds and enlivens even the normally grey and unyielding countenance of the slate. In winter it was good to pull in and look down the valley towards Llangollen, spirits refreshed by the brightness of the clear blue sky and the purity of the skeins of snow and frost. Back on the road the car would weave through the pass and down past the abbey at its foot and each time Alexander would relate – with what degree of historical accuracy could never be ascertained – how the monks would emerge to waylay and rob unsuspecting travellers. Tea and snacks in any one of Llangollen's several tea-shops would follow and there was usually a visit to the large second-hand bookshop before repairing to the town's main hotel for a drink. Once the threesome stopped at the little motor museum which is on the road into Llangollen as one approaches from the Horseshoe Pass. Alexander

166

was entranced by what he found there. His interest in cars was lifelong and he gleefully pointed to old models with their flaring front wings and bug-eyed headlamps and deep, rich chrome and paintwork which he remembered from his youth.

As Frame and Buckingham approached the Ponderosa having left the inquest the unspoken thought passed between them that what they were seeing was what their friend had seen in his very last few minutes on earth. They found the metalled road almost opposite the Ponderosa without difficulty. A couple of hundred yards along it there was a small lay-by and it was here that Alexander had parked his buff-coloured Montego, taken the shopping bag from the passenger seat and began his last, lonely walk. By now the piece of rope that had secured the fence had been replaced by a chain. They climbed the fence and slid uncertainly down the muddy bank of the river, towards the scene of Alexander's death. Why this particular place? they wondered. It was beautiful in its seclusion, but no more so than a dozen other places within easy driving distance. Was it that Alexander and Rosina, before the war, had driven here from Shrewsbury and settling themselves in the little hollow beneath the tree had exchanged kisses or that for Donnie and him it held some special significance? Was the sweetness of the spot not in the undoubted beauty of its aspect, but in the long-remembered kisses of a woman a quarter-of-a-century dead? That will never be known. But the ghost of Alexander Cordell is still at the place, just as it is forever on the mountainside over Blaenavon where in one incandescent moment, the greatest book of the imagination ever to be written in and about Gwent was conceived.